Seeing All Kids
as Readers

Seeing All Kids
as Readers

A New Vision for Literacy in the
Inclusive Early Childhood Classroom

by

Christopher Kliewer, Ph.D.
University of Northern Iowa

·P A U L·H·
BROOKES
PUBLISHING C⁰ ®

Baltimore • London • Sydney

Paul H. Brookes Publishing Co.
Post Office Box 10624
Baltimore, Maryland 21285-0624
USA

www.brookespublishing.com

Typeset by Spearhead Global, Inc., Bear, Delaware.
Manufactured in the United States of America by
Versa Press, Inc., East Peoria, Illinois.

Case studies described in this book are based on the author's actual experiences. In all
instances, names and identifying details have been changed to protect confidentiality.

Supported in part by the U.S. Department of Education Grants Nos. H324D010031 and
H324C040213. However, the content does not necessarily reflect the position of the U.S.
Department of Education, and no official endorsement should be inferred.

Excerpts on pages 80, 81, 82, and 83 reprinted with the permission of Simon & Schuster
Adult Publishing Group from TEACHER by Sylvia Ashton-Warner. Copyright © 1963
by Sylvia Ashton-Warner. Copyright renewed © 1991 by Elliot Henderson, Ashton
Henderson, and Jasmine Beveridge.

Library of Congress Cataloguing-in-Publication Data

Kliewer, Christopher.
  Seeing all kids as readers : a new vision for literacy in the inclusive early childhood
classroom / by Christopher Kliewer.
    p.   cm.
  Includes bibliographical references and index.
  ISBN-13: 978-1-55766-901-8 (pbk.)
  ISBN-10: 1-55766-901-5 (pbk.)
  1. Children with disabilities—Education (Early childhood)—United States.
  2. Reading (Early childhood)—United States.   3. Literacy—United States.   I. Title.
  LC4028.5.K58 2008
  371.9'0444—dc22

                                        2008001586

British Library cataloguing in Publication data are available from the British Library.

2012   2011   2010   2009   2008

10   9   8   7   6   5   4   3   2   1

Contents

About the Author

Christopher Kliewer, Ph.D., Professor, Department of Special Education, University of Northern Iowa, Cedar Falls, Iowa 50614

Dr. Kliewer is a professor of special education at the University of Northern Iowa, where he teaches graduate and undergraduate classes on inclusive education and qualitative research methods. His own qualitative research is focused on the literacy development of young children with significant developmental disabilities who are schooled in inclusive early childhood programs. Since 2001, his research has been supported through U.S. Department of Education research grants. His publications have appeared in the *Harvard Educational Review*, *American Educational Research Journal*, and the *Teachers College Record* among numerous other sociological and educational research venues.

Acknowledgments

I greatly appreciate the willingness to take a risk (and stick with me!) on the part of Rebecca Lazo at Brookes Publishing Co. I also am indebted to Glinda Hill at the U.S. Department of Education who has patiently overseen two research grants (Nos. H324D010031 and H324C040213) out of which this book emerged. The grants have allowed me to spend countless hours in inclusive early childhood centers learning about literacy for all children.

The Jowonio School in Syracuse, New York, is a magical inclusive spot composed of incredible educators, families, and young children. I was first a teacher at Jowonio, and now I wander the halls as a researcher. Thanks so much to the administration, teachers, families, and children.

My understanding of young children's literacy has been influenced through conversations (actual, virtual, and otherwise) with a number of colleagues. I greatly appreciate the energy brought to this project by: Anita Freezman, Janet Sauer, Jamie Burke, Donna Raschke, Paula Kluth, Jodi Meyer-Mork, Pam Johnson, Linda Mae Fitzgerald, Ellen Barnes, Sue Etscheidt, Tony Gabriele, Kathy Klein, Christi Kasa-Hendrickson, Jillian McCarthy, Amy Staples, Emily Barrett, Beth Snyder, Val Dolezal, David Landis, Steve Drake, the Savareses, Sheree Burke, Marilyn Busch, Scot Danforth, and Gunther Kress.

I am thrilled that my parents, Ken and Kathy, have remained so intertwined with my life and work.

Thanks much to our bartenders and friends, Bea and KT.

I am deeply indebted to the absolute originality of educator Zan Currin. Her influence is severe to profound! And, as always, none of this research could ever have occurred without the energy of my mentor and friend, Doug Biklen.

For Angie,
who has loved me through Chapter 4
and so many other complexities

Introduction

This book is based on a series of *ethnographic research studies* that I have conducted since the mid-1990s that explore the *literate development* of *young children with significant developmental disabilities* in *inclusive early childhood education programs.* That mouthful of a sentence requires some elucidation beginning with its italicized ending and moving backward to its italicized beginning.

I define *inclusive early childhood education programs* as center-based classrooms where young children with and without disabilities actively participate together as full and valued members of the community. Historically, children with disabilities have been educationally segregated from their typically developing peers beginning in the earliest years of preschool. My interest is focused on those programs that have left segregation behind and are intent on creating responsive, constructivist environments for all children.

In 2001, the U.S. Department of Education began, and has continued, funding my studies through grants (Nos. H324D10031 and H324C040213). The generous resources provided have allowed me to spend hundreds of hours in nearly 30 inclusive classrooms ranging from toddler rooms through first grade. Add to that number the classrooms involved in my work prior to 2001, and the ideas presented in this book are based on the literate dynamics of approximately 50 inclusive early childhood classrooms involving hundreds of students. In addition, I have had the privilege of following 27 children with significant developmental disabilities during a 2-year period and 13 children with significant developmental disabilities for 3 years, which lends a longitudinal depth to this effort.

In choosing classrooms as participating research sites, I looked for a permeating vibrancy and joy. If I am going to spend numerous hours in a location, that location should be a satisfying and energetic place to be! Of course, vibrancy originates as an emanation from the teaching team that then spreads, saturates, and immerses the entire surrounding community of children and their families. Beyond the subjective vibrancy, other factors common among my classroom settings included the following:

1. A range from preschool to kindergarten (although I followed some children into first grade)

2. Inclusive educational environments where children with significant disabilities and those without disabilities were taught together

3. Educational environments with widespread reputations of excellence among their respective communities

4. Active, programwide commitments to a recognizable literacy curriculum that included varying degrees of child discovery, teacher-led instruction, alphabet skills, story reading and writing, pretend play, art, dance, music, symbolism, and so forth

5. Individualized education programs (IEP) and individualized family service plans (IFSP) reflecting recognizable literacy goals for students with significant disabilities, as well as demonstrated teacher commitment to the literate development of children with significant disabilities

6. Parent confirmation of their child's active participation in the general community of the classroom

7. Data maintained by the school in the form of portfolios and various developmental assessments (including specific literacy assessments) tracking student change

Defining *young children with significant developmental disabilities* is somewhat tricky. Different states, and even different districts within a single state, vary in how children are labeled. All children defined in this book as having significant developmental disabilities were students who qualified for special education services under the Individuals with Disabilities Education Improvement Act of 2004 (PL 108-446). Also, they were children who qualified for a significant level of resources in relation to state disbursement patterns because of the presumed degree of disability. Many, but not all, had specific disability diagnoses (e.g., autism spectrum disorder, Down syndrome, cerebral palsy, Rett syndrome). Preschool children, and now older students, however, may receive services with a generic label (e.g., developmental disability [DD], entitled individual [EI]).

In addition, every participating child with significant developmental disabilities had been assessed on formal developmental instruments as having moderate to severe communication and cognitive delays. Communication aside, this did not mean that every child had moderate to severe intellectual disabilities or that teachers or families believed every child had cognitive delays. It referred strictly to an assessment score.

In relation to communication, developmental assessments are singularly focused on speech and its precursors. They are, after all, normative in construction, and the majority (translated into *normal*) path to communicative fluency certainly is dominated by speech. Some of my dozens of participants with significant developmental disabilities did use speech as their primary mode of expression, albeit in limited fashion compared with same-age typically developing peers. Many had little to no recognizable or seemingly useful speech at all. Every one of these participants did struggle with spoken language. With communication struggles, it is very difficult *not* to get measured as having intellectual disabilities on assessments that require in one way or another speech to prove competence.

I use the rest of this book to define (and describe) *literate development* in young children with significant developmental disabilities. Briefly, the vast amount of time I have spent in inclusive early childhood programs has forced me to leave behind conventional models of young children's literacy development, including both emergent literacy and basic skills–phonics. Neither captures the stirring, kaleidoscopic dynamics of actual children in action with symbols and signs. In addition, I have left behind convention to necessarily broaden the idea of literacy. In this regard, I am in good company (e.g., Gardner, 1991; Kress, 1997). As the reader will eventually note, however, I do not address multiple literacies; rather, I theorize multiple symbol and sign systems as one construct of a triadic model of young children's literate profiles, regardless of whether they have significant developmental disabilities.

Finally, the principle ideas in this book are wholly based on ethnographic research. *Ethnography* is a term most closely associated with anthropology, and, like an anthropologist, I entered inclusive early childhood education programs in naïve fashion, intent on uncovering the literate culture of young children in interaction with one another. Several important principles of ethnography guided my efforts. First, I studied *real-world settings*. I was interested in the literate citizenship of young children with significant disabilities, so I *purposefully* (Bogdan & Biklen, 2003) entered into inclusive settings where preschool, kindergarten, and eventually first-grade students with significant disabilities were actively participating in literacy opportunities.

Second, my data was primarily *narrative*. Third, it *was collected using multiple methods historically associated with ethnography and phenomenology*. I conducted participant observations in the classrooms, interviews with participating adults, and systematic collection of documents associated with the contexts under study. I wrote field notes following observations that included interpretive memos. In essence, field notes tell the story of the observation. I have more than 20 hours of transcribed or described video footage from the classrooms, and I commonly recorded and transcribed interviews.

Fourth, my analysis of the data was *interpretive and grounded in the narrative data*. I read field notes in depth to uncover emergent themes or aspects of the settings that occurred over and over again. From themes I developed coding categories that have now become various sections of this book's chapters. Ultimately, analysis was primarily inductive. For instance, I initially was focused on observing children's use of alphabetic text and how children with significant disabilities struggled in this regard (thus acknowledging certain of my preconceived notions and biases). As this book will illustrate, my perceptions of literacy changed through the process of this research.

Fifth, I am concerned that the theory presented herein is *accurately reflective of the settings from which the theory is derived*. The idea of triangulation as a form of validity in ethnography is a poorly defined one. Its origins exist in navigational methods in which an unknown point can be determined by the use of two known vertices. Loosely translated into interpretive design, multiple data points can bring us to previously unknown ways of looking at the world. Here I submit ideas of literacy based on a vast array of systematic observations conducted since 2001 in nearly 30 classrooms involving hundreds of children. I have previously published my ideas, albeit in truncated fashion, in numerous highly respected peer-reviewed research journals, including the *Harvard Educational Review*, the *Teachers College Record*, and the *American Educational Research Journal*.   •

CONTENT SUMMARY

Chapter 1 introduces the construct of local understanding as fundamental to young children's literacy (Kliewer & Biklen, 2007). *Local understanding* is the capacity to recognize the intelligence, imagination, and drive to make sense of the surrounding world within all children, *and* it is the structuring of thoughtful, inclusive educational contexts that foster, deepen, and expand children's intelligence, imagination, and sense-making.

In Chapter 2, I contrast my model of the inclusive early childhood literate community with historic and current theoretical descriptions of early literacy that have largely excluded young children with significant developmental disabilities. I also present young children's expressions as residing on a continuum running from the highly communicative to the highly representational. This idea becomes important in Chapter 5.

Chapter 3 briefly describes the three constructs that make up the literate profile of young children. These include the following:

1. Symbolic presence (descriptive of the drive to collaboratively make symbolic sense of the surrounding world)

2. Construction of narratives through which children make meaning

3. Generation of symbol or sign systems from which narratives are crafted

I then present some descriptions from 2 days of observation in one particular inclusive classroom. These vignettes serve to illustrate the literate profile of young children with and without significant developmental disabilities.

In Chapter 4, I elaborate on children's symbolic presence, narrative construction, and symbol systems. I explain the dynamic interaction across the three constructs and discuss the tenuous relationship young children with significant developmental disabilities have experienced with conventional models of literacy.

Chapter 5 introduces the four literacy currents that promote the connectedness of children with significant developmental disabilities to the surrounding literate community. I offer both theoretical description and practical examples of the developing sophistication with literacy on the part of young participants involved in my research.

In Chapter 6, the conclusion, I synthesize and reiterate important components of the previous chapters. I also discuss literacy as a civil right of all children.

Chapter 1

"Dancing to Books"

Local Understanding and
Literate Participation in Early Childhood

Four-year-old Isaac Johansson pulled the children's picture book *Where the Wild Things Are* (Sendak, 1964) from the hands of his teacher, Shayne Robbins. He held it over his head and doubled forward with a shriek of excitement. Ms. Robbins pointed toward the large blue rug and said to Isaac, "Go ahead on over. Bring the book. Everyone needs to get to the rug."

Sixteen 4- and 5-year-old students began to make their way to the morning circle. Most meandered willingly; however, several protests and groans of discontent arose from a group of four boys who had built an intricate web of roads out of wooden blocks and had crafted complex narratives involving toy cars, police chases, "bad guys," and heroes. Two girls quickly strode to the rug arm in arm, while a third girl, clearly being ostracized, struggled to keep pace.

Isaac's mother watched from near the classroom door. This was Isaac's first day in the Corner Nook classroom at the Shoshone School, an early childhood education center where children with and without disabilities learn together in inclusive classrooms of students who range in age from toddler to kindergarten age. As a researcher focused on the literacy of young children with significant developmental disabilities and those without disabilities, I had spent a great deal of time over several years observing, analyzing, and documenting the culture and practices of various classrooms at the Shoshone School, as well as several other inclusive early childhood programs across several states.

The Corner Nook was the first of my research sites, and I felt very fortunate to be in the room on Isaac's first day.

Isaac's excitement at Ms. Robbins's choice of literature turned to visible trepidation as his mother slipped from the room. He held tightly to his chosen book as if it were a security blanket. He slowly followed the other children toward their places on the rug.

It was already several weeks into the school year. Isaac had started the year in a different program at another school. His initial placement had been in a segregated, self-contained special education classroom designed for children identified as having moderate to severe developmental disabilities. He was born with trisomy 21 (commonly known as Down syndrome), which is a chromosomal anomaly in which the individual is born with three rather than two 21st chromosomes in each of the human body's trillions of cells. Beginning at his first birthday, early intervention special education professionals administered developmental checklists that suggested Isaac had significant cognitive, communicative, and physical delays.

"We weren't that interested in all those tests," Isaac's mother, Bridgett Johansson, explained in a conversation we had about her son. "We didn't know what to do with that information, so we just kept raising him the way we did his sisters [who do not have disabilities]."

By Isaac's second birthday, medical doctors and the early intervention professionals were pressuring the Johanssons to send Isaac to a segregated special education program designed for children with moderate to severe disabilities. When Isaac turned 4 years old, "We went ahead and enrolled him," said his mother.

> We were doing exactly what we were told would be best for him. When you have no clue, I guess you eventually listen to experts.

Isaac's parents described the segregated program as devoid of recognizable preschool opportunities, including literacy activities. Isaac's mother said, "No picture books, no children's books at all, no paint, no pretend kitchen, no dolls."

Isaac's father interjected,

> Nothing that you think of when you think of nursery school. Nothing like what his sisters had…. No kid in the program actually spoke. Isaac had the most speech, and he hardly speaks.

Isaac's parents reported that, approximately 6 weeks into the school year, when they raised the issue of language models, reading, writing, painting, and other recognized aspects of a quality general early childhood program, their queries were immediately shut down.

Mrs. Johansson tersely recalled, "We were told that other functional skills were a priority."

Isaac remained in the segregated program for approximately 6 more weeks before his frustrated parents decided to move him to another school. "He was nothing but a defect to them," Isaac's mother said. "I was set to home school, but then we heard about Shoshone."

An opening occurred in an inclusive classroom taught by Ms. Robbins at Shoshone School. The paperwork for admissions was completed, and prior to Isaac's first day entering the classroom, Ms. Robbins made two visits to Isaac's home. She wanted to meet the family and ease Isaac's transition into the new preschool. From those visits, Ms. Robbins learned about Isaac's passion for books, particularly by children's author Maurice Sendak, who wrote *Where the Wild Things Are*.

In a later discussion about her teaching, Ms. Robbins explained,

> I knew Isaac would be a little scared at first, being the new kid in the class, so I knew we had to do something he was comfortable with [and] excited about. So we made the theme of the week into the *Wild Things!*

The classic story is about a boy named Max who is sent to his room, where he falls asleep and dreams of sailing to a land inhabited by monsters.

IMPLEMENTING LOCAL UNDERSTANDING

In their sense of Isaac as a rightful and able participant in the full breadth of a quality preschool experience, and in their efforts to make that sense a deeply meaningful reality for Isaac, both his parents and Shoshone personnel demonstrated what I refer to as *local understanding* (Kliewer & Biklen, 2007). Local understanding moves beyond the common dehumanizing, distant, or institutionalized labels, definitions, and expectations historically associated with significant developmental disability. For example, Ms. Robbins's decision to use a favorite book as a way of connecting Isaac to his new community demonstrated her understanding and unqualified acceptance of the power of literacy in Isaac's life.

Ms. Robbins's belief in Isaac's literate presence contrasts institutional understanding of significant disability. The American Psychiatric Association's (2004) *Diagnostic and Statistical Manual of Mental Disorders, Fourth Edition, Text Revision* describes individuals with *severe mental retardation* in a way that diminishes real literate possibility for these individuals.

Local understanding envisions an individual's citizenship or right to full community participation, literate and otherwise, and crafts responsive contexts within which active citizenship might be fostered and realized. The visibility of citizenship is enhanced in meaningful, thoughtfully structured contexts. As a child's participatory capacities increase in sophistication, so too does the sense of his or her citizenship. Through local understanding, the Johanssons and Ms. Robbins and her staff realized Isaac's rightful place in the swirl of the inclusive preschool community and, through dialogue with one another, acted to make the Corner Nook conducive to his valued and meaningful participation. Local understanding is of fundamental importance throughout this book, not because it is a method of instruction or a set of approaches in reading and writing; rather, it is the cultural genesis to literacy. Local understanding is a moral endeavor through which the literate potential of all children, with or without disabilities, is recognized.

ENCOURAGING LITERATE PARTICIPATION

Continuing with my observation of Isaac on his first day in the Corner Nook at Shoshone School, I watched as he apprehensively made his way to the blue rug, the book held tight against his chest. He stood and watched as other children wandered across the rug, eyeing smaller carpet pieces that each had a strip of masking tape bearing a name. The students recognized their names and sat on the appropriate carpet squares. One of three assistant teachers in the classroom, Janelle King, saw Isaac looking somewhat befuddled.

"Whoops," she said. "I was supposed to get you a carpet spot. I'm sorry Isaac." She grabbed an unused piece of carpet from the remaining pile and stuck a strip of tape across it. Kneeling next to Isaac, Ms. King said, "Okay, let's put your name on this—your own brand new carpet spot. Let me write I-S-A-A-C." She slowly enunciated the letters as she wrote them in their capital form. She used her hands to cover all but the double A in the name. "Look," she said. "You have an A and an A right in a row!" Isaac smiled.

Teachers use the carpet squares to help the students develop a sense of structure and boundary during group times. Ms. King said, "Go ahead and have a seat now, Isaac." He remained standing.

Ms. Robbins had just arrived at the rug carrying several commercially available stuffed dolls representing Max and several of the *Wild Things* monsters. "May I have the book?" she asked Isaac. He turned away from her, protecting his treasured literature. "I tell you what," Ms. Robbins said. "I'll swap you. You can hold Max, and I'll hold the book."

"I want Max!" cried out Trevor, a 4-year-old student.

Ms. Robbins said, "We'll let Isaac have Max. It's his first day."

Trevor shrugged and said, "Yeah." Trevor's interest affected Isaac, who handed the book to Ms. Robbins. She gave him the stuffed Max figure. Isaac plopped onto the carpet spot.

Trevor leaned in close and touched his nose to the Max doll in Isaac's hand. "Hi, Max. Hi, Max," he repeated several times in a silly fashion while shaking his head back and forth. Isaac smiled and shook his own head, much like Trevor.

Ms. Robbins took her usual place on the carpet. Behind her, taped to the wall, was a large sheet of paper with a description of the class visit to the post office. The children had dictated the narrative a few days earlier. She opened the picture book and began reading about the character Max committing various acts of misbehavior, including chasing his dog with a fork before being sent to bed without dinner. Her students listened intently to the familiar story as she showed the pictures slowly around the group.

Emily, a 4-year-old seated near Isaac, noting the picture yelled out, "Max shouldn't run with a fork!"

Patrick, also 4 years old, shared, "My daddy sent me to my room."

Ms. Robbins paused to ask, "For running with a fork?"

Patrick said, "Nawww."

Ms. Robbins dropped the book to her lap and asked, "Well, what did you do?"

Patrick looked sheepish with hands drawn to his mouth and would only say, "He was just really mad."

Ms. Robbins and the three assistant teachers and a visiting speech-language therapist laughed, but the children stared at Patrick, many with distant gazes as though they were looking right through Patrick into their own parents' tempers. Thadeus, who had just turned 5 years old, shouted out, "My sister got grounded."

"Got what?" another child asked.

Yet another child, on her knees and falling toward the center of the circle, blurted, "I'se grounded."

Ms. Robbins broke in, "Okay, okay. We're all going to get in trouble sometimes. Sometimes even I get in trouble."

Isaac sat amid this engaging interaction, the stuffed Max character in his arms, gleefully waiting each turn of the page. When Ms. Robbins turned to the illustrations in which the character Max engages in a dancing "rumpus" with the wild things, Isaac could no longer contain himself. He leapt to his feet and began dancing along with the picture that covered two full pages in the book.

Ms. Robbins laughed and said, "Isaac has the rumpusing moves! Who else can rumpus?"

In a flash, nearly all of the children were on their feet spinning and twirling. I observed with awe and wonder as Isaac led the giggling, shrieking children in dance, having never considered the possibility of dancing to books at all.

Amazingly, within 1 hour of starting school in the Corner Nook at Shoshone, local understanding had transformed Isaac from a child presumed by numerous experts to require a segregated program devoid of children's literature and other imaginative and creative opportunities into a child recognized as part of the literate culture of the classroom. His interests, garnered first by Ms. Robbins's interaction with his parents during visits to Isaac's home, actually directed the choice of readings and related activities, and his understanding of the text ultimately led to a whole-group dance to the story.

Beyond the group reading time that week, Ms. Robbins and her colleagues developed a variety of learning centers in the classroom that extended from various other storybooks by author Maurice Sendak. Among these, for instance, was his picture book *In the Night Kitchen* (1970) in which a character named Mickey wanders across a dreamlike cityscape made up of kitchen materials, including containers and utensils. The teaching team had the children bring empty boxes and cans from their kitchens at home, and the class constructed its own "Night Kitchen" out of the containers, other boxes, construction paper, paints, and so forth.

During one center time, I observed Isaac gluing an oatmeal box to a flat piece of cardboard with the assistance of an adult. Using a thick brush, he then painted broad, irregular green lines on the cardboard. The adult asked, "Are you painting a road? A road goes past your oatmeal building?" Isaac continued painting without a clearly discernable response.

What stood out about this interaction at the learning center, similar to the *Wild Things* dance, was the seemingly organic assumption of symbolic sense ascribed to Isaac's actions by those around him. His blotching of paint was imbued with symbolic, abstract, and metaphoric meaning (e.g., The paint is like a road. Isaac is representing a road). That Isaac had a story to tell and the means to tell it was, in this environment of local understanding, never in question!

THE GENESIS OF LOCAL UNDERSTANDING

Local understanding emerged in my ethnographies as an educational variant of the ideas underlying the theoretical construct *local knowledge* described in the work of anthropologist Clifford Geertz (1983). He observed non-Western cultural settings in which individuals demonstrated nonscientific but highly sophisticated, rational, and intricate knowledge of a problem or need based on a deep, intimate understanding of the specific context. Local knowledge has been studied across a range of phenomena, including, for instance, highly accurate weather prediction (Rancoli, Ingram, & Kirshen, 2002) and complex soil-preserving crop rotation patterns (Gray & Morant, 2003) on the part of rural villagers unschooled in formal meteorology or agronomy and conservation.

Local knowledge as a situated form of understanding, although certainly not absent in Western cultures (e.g., the mother as expert on her own children, the local car mechanic tweaking a sensitive carburetor in an engine he has maintained for years), is of a decidedly lower status compared with technical-rational (sometimes referred to as *scientific*) knowledge (Kliewer & Drake, 1998). Born of the enlightenment, technical-rational elucidations seek an objective detachment from any specific situation in their manifest drive toward universal and absolute responses to the puzzles exhibited by the empirical world. Even my two examples of local knowledge holdouts within Western rationalism, the mother and the local auto mechanic, are under siege. Expertise in parenting is perceptually shifting from the mother to "parenting experts." Meanwhile, the carburetor has vanished, and the mechanic is becoming one who, in strangely clean coveralls, plugs the engine into a digitally omnipotent computer that sifts and interprets the data and spits out the universally applicable diagnostics.

In a drive to mimic the natural sciences, what I call *physics envy*, local knowledge has largely been criticized or ignored in the psychological and social sciences. In fact, the history of these fields is often one of self-consciously running from local forms of understanding (Kliewer & Fitzgerald, 2001). Research and theorizing become efforts toward "grand textures of cause and effect" (Geertz, 1983, p. 6) as deduced through "laws-and-causes social physics" (p. 5) to ecumenically account for individual and collective human action. This effort at grand theory, however, has failed within the psychological and social sciences "to produce the triumphs of prediction, control, and testability that had for so long been promised in its name" (p. 3).

The drift and direction of the psychological and social sciences has, in turn, dragged along its applied counterparts in the fields associated with disability and education. Applied psychological, human service, and educational sciences create a detached human cosmology of impairment through their disability labels, classifications, and categories. In contrast, local understanding recognizes that the behavior, communication, and intent of children with developmental disabilities do not have built-in, universal meanings. Rather, it is understood that cultural meanings are built up in the swirling, collective, interpretive, and imaginative dialogues of a particular community. This is what Geertz (1983) referred to as dialogic "local frames of awareness" (p. 6) or as "accent—vernacular characterizations of what happens connected with vernacular imaginings of what can" (p. 215). Local understanding is the communal recognition that educational value and participation may be ascribed and enacted around a specific child, whereas history has primarily supported an abstract dehumanization and segregation.

A child such as Isaac, with extraordinarily limited speech, a somewhat awkward gait, and the diagnosis of trisomy 21, may be considered by disability professionals from an impairment perspective. Indeed, while Isaac was still a toddler, professionals assessed him, scored him, and separated him in rituals of practice that effectively reduce the whole of a child to the deficit contours associated with various categories of impairment. These common rituals of expertise embody what Geertz (1983) described as "the machinery of distant ideas" (p. 4). In the arena of disability, this machinery is built from the behavioral and psychometric branches of psychological science and the bureaucracy of human services. The distant frames commonly overwhelm other forms of understanding a child as they have generally come to dominate explanatory and regulatory discourses of disability.

Seemingly unavoidable consequences of stratification often await children labeled as having severe disabilities, including segregation into special education classrooms that commonly lack thoughtful or recognizable academic opportunities, including, most importantly, access to literacy (Erickson & Koppenhaver, 1995; Kliewer & Biklen, 2001; Mirenda, 2003). In the Shoshone School, however, the collective local understanding of Isaac and other children with significant disabilities challenged the medical and psychological machinery of disability, segregation, and aliteracy by realizing Isaac's immediate competence as a literate citizen and his ability to grow in literate sophistication.

Chapter 2

"It's About Making Sense"

Citizenship in the Inclusive Early Childhood Literate Community

At the start of my literacy studies in the mid-1990s, I initially focused on what I now view as a rather rigid delineation of the meaning of literacy for young children with significant developmental disabilities—their direct interaction with alphabetic text most often occurs (or at least is most easily visible) under an adult's control. From the data scenario on Isaac's first day in the Corner Nook classroom at the inclusive Shoshone School (see Chapter 1), evidence of how this is a limiting definition may have included, for instance, Isaac's recognition of the book *Where the Wild Things Are*, the use of written names on the rug squares, the children's exposure to the story read, and the post office story dictated by the children. Conventionally, literacy remains strictly aligned with alphabetic print that allows an author to systematically encode ideas and convey those ideas across time and space to an audience able to decode the text.

During the first decades of the 20th century, when nursery school, preschool, and formal child care originated, the primary discourse of literacy in early childhood education captured young children as passive recipients of written texts read to them (Crawford, 1995). Only after beginning first grade were children considered mature enough to learn the skills of decoding, then encoding, printed language. Since the 1960s, this discourse of passive preparation in early childhood has slowly but generally been subverted by more recent theories of literacy

development. This has largely occurred across two competing movements—*emergent literacy* and *basic skills–phonics*.

In the late 1960s, a developmental model described as *emergent
literacy* focused on written language as *naturally* developing in conjunction and intertwined with the emergence of spoken language
(Teale & Sulzby, 1986). In this framework, early literacy for young children was a pedagogical concern only to the degree that educators
could create interactive, symbolic, and print- and story-rich environments through which the young child's organic capacities might
emerge in stable, Piagetian stage–like fashion as a foundation for later
written language skills.

For years, the principal American professional and advocacy
organization on early childhood issues and policy, the National Association for the Education of Young Children (NAEYC), refrained from
identifying literacy as a distinct category of concern for young children.
Taking a stance aligned with emergent literacy, NAEYC viewed its
advocacy of thoughtful constructivist and child-centered curricula
orientations to be sufficient. According to this logic, as with all developmental domains and subdomains, a child's literate growth would
naturally occur when provided with a rich, developmentally appropriate context. In 1998, however, in response to a growing back-to-
basics movement decrying the state of reading competence in
American students, the NAEYC felt compelled to issue a position statement on literacy.

The NAEYC's literacy treatise, drafted in cooperation with the
International Reading Association (IRA & NAEYC, 1998), was an effort
to affirm its commitment to developmentally appropriate early childhood practices, including emergent literacy. It stated that prior to the
introduction of formal reading programs, preschool children

> Begin to acquire some basic understandings of the concepts about liter-
> acy and its functions. Children learn to use symbols, combining their oral
> language, pictures, print, and play into a coherent mixed medium and
> creating and communicating meanings in a variety of ways. (1998, p. 3)

As such, "Reading and writing acquisition is conceptualized better as
a developmental continuum" (1998, p. 3).

At the time, the galvanized back-to-basics movement grouped
emergent literacy with its primary nemesis, *whole language* reading
instruction, in the elementary school. Both, it felt, were at the heart of
the problems in public school classrooms across the United States
(McGuiness, 1997). Perhaps because of the climate and sociopolitical
pressures, the joint statement strayed from what had previously been

defined as developmentally appropriate support of certain nonconstructivist approaches, including 1) direct instruction for preschoolers in the alphabetic principle (i.e., the understanding of a systematic relationship between sound and letters); 2) linguistic awareness as the root of phonemic awareness and developed through teacher-led choral chants and rhyming; and 3) exercises in phonemic awareness, but only after young children "have learned some letter names, shapes, and sounds" (IRA & NAEYC, 1998, p. 3).

As a result of the political successes of the back-to-basics movement at the early childhood level, the *basic skills–phonics* model replaced emergent literacy as the predominant policy description of early literacy development in young children (Kliewer & Biklen, 2007). Within this framework, written language was considered a system of externally delineated symbols and rules that children must be taught through systematic, direct instruction and drill along a linear trajectory in phonemic, graphemic, and orthographic skills (Adams, 1990, 2001). Early literacy was an entirely pedagogical concern as it was considered an acquired product of teacher-organized, highly structured activities. These activities for preschool-age children included direct instruction, phonics drills, and pages of skill worksheet exercises that previously were used only after the child entered elementary school.

Soon after I began directing my ethnographic gaze toward printed language in preschools and kindergartens, I experienced the need to shed what I now term my rigid or conventional sense of literacy and expand beyond the explanatory models of emergent literacy or basic skills. This need to augment my focus beyond a child's direct experience with alphabetic text, whether drilled by teachers or naturally occurring within a rich environment, arose out of the grounded theory I was generating on young children's citizenship in the inclusive early childhood literate community. The accumulating evidence suggested that the literate profile of a child's citizenship was dynamically composed of a triadic set of intertwined constructs that included

1. The child's symbolic presence—his or her extraordinary motivation to imagine, make sense of the surrounding world, and develop a connectedness with others

2. The child's crafting of stories and narratives in interaction with others through which meaning and relationships are constructed

3. The child's multiple systems of signs and symbols created and enacted for the development of stories and narratives

This triadic literate profile evolved from observations of children with and without disabilities in inclusive sites, in-depth discussions with master early childhood inclusion teachers who oversaw the children's efforts to construct meaning, an emerging sense of local understanding that guided these thoughtful programs, and interactions with the work of other language researchers.

Ms. Robbins, Isaac's teacher, told me in a discussion addressing the idea of early literacy that "It's about making sense." She hesitated, then repeated,

> It's about making sense. It's kids being able to...have something to tell, and to be able to tell it and hear it in a lot of ways so that it's understood.

In these terms of *making sense* and having *something to tell,* Ms. Robbins emphasized children's constructions of meaning (or making sense) and expression and communication as key facets of literacy. In a later interview, Ms. Robbins noted,

> It's really all about literacy. There's very little we do that's not literacy related, even when it doesn't look exactly like reading the way you and I look when we sit down and read a book.

Similarly, Shirley Kehoe, lead teacher at the inclusive Prairie View preschool explained to me that

> [Literacy is] taking the kids seriously at every level—their experiences they come with, their emotions, their interests, their meanings. You put them in a setting where all those things are acknowledged and built on, and they all realize they have something to say, and they say it in so many ways. Sometimes with their voice, but just as often in a lot of other ways. And their expressiveness just grows, and they start to read—each other, books, art.

Rather than only emphasizing children's interactions with adult-controlled printed language, teachers involved in my studies were equating early literacy for young children with ideas and phrases, such as "Making sense," "The realization of something to say," and "Taking kids seriously, including their experiences, emotions, interests, meanings." Early literacy involved interactions with alphabetic text generally, but it also, according to my interviews, involved the following:

- Observations and analyses
- Dimensions composing the triadic early literacy profile involving children's symbolic presence or motivation to imagine, make meaning, and connect with one another

- Children crafting stories and narratives through which meaning is constructed

- Children's development of visual, orthographic (e.g., alphabetic), and tactile sign and symbol systems for the expression or interpretation of stories and narratives

YOUNG CHILDREN'S EXPRESSION ON A CONTINUUM

Research on children's early language is commonly divided into the explosion of the spoken word during the first few years of a child's life versus the seemingly more laborious trek into the written word or lettered representation of language (commonly called *literacy*) (Gardner, 1991). My own research, however, following the work of Kress (1997), placed young children's engagement with symbols or sign systems (including speech and traditional literacy) on a continuum running from the highly communicative in intent to the highly representational in intent. The image of a continuum suggests that neither end, communication nor representation, is necessarily exclusive of the other; rather, young children emphasize one or the other in their expressions of narrative.

On the communicative side, children make use of whatever symbols and materials are available to most aptly, efficiently, or clearly convey the narratives of thought, emotion, and ideas to an audience. At this end of the continuum, the audience is of central and equal importance to the child. To communicate with an audience, young children rely on speech as their primary modus operandi. Certainly tears, laughter, fists, and other forms of expression imbued with symbolic value are liberally included, but speech is the central and most apt sign system involved in communication. Indeed, if a young child primarily relies on any mode or system other than speech for communicative purposes, he or she will be labeled as having a disability.

As described in Chapter 1, several children at the Shoshone School connected with the main character, Max, being sent to his room as a punishment during the circle time reading of *Where the Wild Things Are*. These children wanted to share or communicate experiences that connected with the story and, therefore, began to blurt out, or voice, their own narratives. Isaac, whose speech was extremely limited and difficult to decipher, was in a sense left out of this interactive moment.

On the representational side, children make use of whatever symbols and materials are available to most aptly, wholly, and satisfactorily express thought, emotion, and ideas to one's self. At this end of the continuum, the primary audience of concern is the child him- or herself. Certainly representational expression may involve speech in the form of self-talk, but in early childhood the symbols and signs of fantasy and dramatic play, drawing and painting, dance, movement, sculpture and clay modeling, and early efforts with alphabetic writing are also prevalent. Grouped together, I refer to these visual, orthographic, and tactile symbols and sign systems dominating the representational edge of the early childhood expressive continuum as *literacy*. Emphasizing representation does not exclude communication, and the continuum image suggests that the young child may slide dramatically or by degree toward the communicative end of the continuum (or vice versa) at any given moment. When Isaac rose to "rumpus" with *Where the Wild Things Are,* it appeared he had less of a communicative intent in mind and more the need to express his utter joy. However, his representational symbol, the dance, ultimately had communicative implications.

In my research involving young children with significant developmental disabilities, I focus on those modes of visual, orthographic, or tactile expression, what I term *literacy*, most closely associated with the representational end of the early childhood expressive continuum. In my earliest study on children with significant developmental disabilities and inclusive education (Kliewer, 1995), I quickly realized that written language in one form or another made up a vast amount of the elementary, and even a good portion of the preschool, curriculum. At this point in my career, I still rigidly associated literacy only with a child's use of or interaction with the alphabet. Teachers who developed ways of supporting the participation of children with disabilities in the written language agenda of school seemed to succeed in fostering what I described as a child's *citizenship*. This did not mean that every child I identified as a citizen had conventional literacy skills but that they were supported in imaginative fashion within the written dimensions of school. Other children who were less thoughtfully supported were cast into what I referred to as the devalued status of *squatter* or segregated *alien* (see also Kliewer, 1998a, 1998b).

From the beginning I saw the importance of opening written language opportunities to students at risk of disability segregation. As I continued to ethnographically examine young children's skills with print, it became increasingly clear that these initial efforts on the part of children without significant disabilities tended to be focused on telling a story in a manner that satisfied the child him- or herself. If the child wanted to share the story with an audience, he or she generally translated the early writing into speech.

In addition to early orthographic efforts at writing, I noted that young children, both with and without disabilities, made use of other types of symbols, representational signs, and whole modalities to capture stories. Indeed, efforts with print were generally embedded within, and subservient to, these other symbolic modes. What of the children's dress up; imaginative object use; molding of clay; dramatic gestures during fantasy play; or complex drawings made with representational figures, squiggles, and fantastic colors and abstract shapes? Even in their spontaneity, I knew these all had cultural meaning and communal social history devoured by children who transformed them into a unique shape based on individual experience, interest, passion, and opportunity. Children's lettered representations (i.e., their constructive use of the alphabet) grew out of and in turn advanced these other sign systems as the breadth and depth of children's symbolic presence, and narrative structuring increased in sophistication, representational capacity, and complexity. Were all these forms of literacy? They certainly appeared vital to young children's representational meaning making.

The idea of early literacy continued to diverge and diversify in my research as I documented how written language itself seemed to be going through dramatic cultural changes, even as I was trying to pin down how young children became literate (Kliewer et al., 2004). For instance, what had been the historical purview of lettered representation was quickly becoming extremely visual and pictorial. A quick glance at the *Dick and Jane* early readers from the 1960s versus early readers used in kindergarten and first grade at the beginning of the millennium demonstrates a dramatic shift toward fewer words on any given page and much more information contained in charts, cartoons, and graph-like representations.

This trend, of course, extends into adulthood. Contrast the *USA Today* or a current issue of *The New York Times* with an issue of *The New York Times* from 30 years ago. Much more information is now encoded and conveyed in charts, graphs, brief captions, and cartoons. In the older papers, there were many more words to a page. Certainly this represents shifts that have come with the rise of visual media.

Kress (1997) pointed out, "We are, it seems, entering a new age of the image, a new age of hieroglyphics" (p. xvii). Thus, to study children's early literacy also requires the study of visual symbolic modalities that support, replace, or enhance text and are themselves supported and enhanced by surrounding text. Indeed, the border between the two, text and pictorial representations, is often nonexistent.

In addition to visual forms of representation replacing what was once either unsaid or contained in text, written language (or conventional literacy) is now in a further state of change as it loses its monopoly on, and even association with, relative permanence and the capacity to reach large audiences across time and space. These changes in permanence began with Morse, Bell, and Edison who attacked it from the communicative side of the expressive continuum by sending speech (and ultimately images) far away from the speaker in distance and time through wire and recording. Whereas spoken language is now more permanent and dispersible, written language has in many ways become more fleeting and speechlike. Cyberspace is an obvious example. People encode chains of digital text and instant messages that are intended to accomplish what spoken conversation did prior to the popularity of these electronic methods.

Similarly, young children produce a vast array of signs and symbols (e.g., during dramatic play) that for a fleeting moment are made visually accessible for others to read and interpret before they are morphed into subsequent chains of signs and body movements. These observable symbols and signs are early literate forms connected to future lettered representations and are becoming increasingly spontaneous and fleeting in our culture.

Recognition of the embodiment of pictorial and ethereal symbols and signs within the construct of literacy has led me to an emphasis on young children's creation and engagement with visual, orthographic, and/or tactile sign and symbol systems. These modalities are centrally relevant and coalescent of a young child's early literacy. I do not use the term *multiple literacies*, but I do speak of multiple symbol and sign systems that compose the dimension of the triadic early literate profile through which a child's citizenship is formed.

Ms. Robbins rattled off a list of visual, orthographic, or tactile sign and symbol modalities that are at least partially distinct from the speech used by children in her classroom to capture, fix, convey, and interpret narratives. "It's all the signing [sign language] we do," she explained. "The art, music, pictures, the symbols, all the symbols and tools we use in play, and of course the stories we write and read and perform, like the skits we put on, books we act out. It's [literacy] everywhere."

For young children with significant developmental disabilities, this broadened understanding of literacy has developmental and democratic implications. For instance, as described thoroughly in Chapter 5, struggles with communication in general and spoken language specifically are common to the label of significant developmental disabilities in early childhood (Mirenda, 2003). Every child in this study who qualified for special education resources due to labels associated with moderate to severe developmental disabilities had specific and serious dilemmas with speech. Personnel related to the field of augmentative and alternative communication (AAC) for children and adults with developmental disabilities craft communication methods that allow the individual to express him- or herself in an understandable fashion. Most often these methods, whether involving high, low, or no technology, include visual, orthographic, or tactile symbol systems (Koppenhaver & Erickson, 2003). Thus, denial of literacy for young children with significant developmental disabilities is similar to denial of voice.

Bridging developmental and democratic implications, I previously pointed out that automatic exclusion from the literate opportunities and agendas of school also likely causes segregation from the general community of school. Children with moderate to significant developmental disabilities who find themselves in segregated special education classrooms or even whole segregated schools, compared with similar students in inclusive settings, consistently demonstrate lower achievement in traditional areas of literacy and numeracy, reduced communicative and language capacities, worse social skills, and less competence in the community (Kliewer, 1998c). Segregation demolishes human potential. Furthermore, automatic denial of literate opportunities accompanied by segregation, which is so often experienced by people with significant developmental disabilities, diminishes an individual's potential for community participation. When an individual is cut from the community for reasons associated with the cultural devaluation of disability, so too is the richness of experience that person might have brought to the community. We all lose, and our democracy suffers for it.

Implications of a Broadened Sense of Literacy

The active, collaborative, and imaginative construction of meaning on the part of children—as well as their motivated, interactive development of narratives and the multiple visual, orthographic, and tactile sign and symbol systems through which narratives are caught and conveyed—moved from a peripheral or aftereffect of literacy acquisition to the epicenter of my studies on initial literacy experiences. I began to understand this triadic literacy profile as the source of a child's valued literate citizenship. The general inclusive early childhood setting was a terrain of (potential) signs and symbols on which story or narrative could be captured, fixed, and conveyed or interpreted by children motivated to imagine, make meaning of their surrounding world, and connect with one another. The construction of meaning through the production and reproduction of sign and symbol systems led children and their supporting adults to organize, compose, and construct a dynamic, valued, and democratic literate community within the context of the inclusive classroom. The use of the term *democratic* embodies the frame of local understanding in which no child is excluded, and every child is perceived to be capable of contributing to the valued connectedness of the community.

Within every inclusive early childhood literate community I have studied, print or written language and the skills its production and interpretation require retain a unique and righteously powerful position among the sign systems potentially available to children's meaning making. In this work, I maintain a deep interest in children's performance with alphabetic text. This interest, however, is necessarily augmented by my earlier-described recognition of the importance of other visual and tactile sign systems in the early literacy of young children with and without disabilities. "Few would question," Gardner (1991) pointed out, "the choice of language as the symbol system par excellence, but it is important to underscore the potency of other symbol systems" (p. 56). Gardner explained,

> Much knowledge is apprehended and communicated through gesture and other paralinguistic means. Depiction of aspects of the world through drawings, constructions in blocks or clay, or other iconic vehicles is a symbolic avenue of great significance in early childhood. Variations of pretense play and rule-governed play are favorite pursuits everywhere. An introduction to the concept of quantity and to the names and operations associated with numbers is part and parcel of the first years of childhood. And various customs, rituals, games, and other social interactions are rife with symbols of various sorts, whose meanings are at least partially accessible to—and in all probability highly potent for—the preschool child. (1991, pp. 56–57)

A certain pragmatic implication of my theoretical shift toward a broadened and dynamic sense of a literate community meant focusing on social interactions, behavior, and symbolic expressions that I previously would have relegated to other domains. Local understanding became inextricably intertwined with the idea of early childhood literate citizenship. For instance, in the opening scenario describing Isaac's initial experiences in the Corner Nook classroom, my interests necessarily expanded beyond just his involvement with printed language under adult guidance. I wanted to know how this child who had been professionally relegated, as his mother described it, to the status of "defect" was understood in his new school as having a complex symbolic presence. This meant adults and peers recognized literate citizenship in Isaac's motivated drive and potential to imagine and make sense out of the experiences of others and to organize his own experiences into symbolic patterns and shapes—what I call *narratives*—that might be captured, fixed, and shared through various sign and symbolic tools of connectedness. In essence, how did Isaac ascend so dramatically from a child perceived as void of stories to one filled with stories and a motivated interest to connect with the stories of others?

The Child's Emotional Connection to Literacy

Within this framework of local understanding and participation in a valued literate community, my ethnographic radar honed in on Isaac's perceived capacity to have a favorite author and to have an emotional attachment to particular storybooks. I wanted to better understand motivated or purposeful representational actions and communication that flowed from this emotional connection. These representational and communicative efforts included, for instance, his resistance to giving up *Where the Wild Things Are* when his teacher first asked for the book and his lead in dancing like the characters in the book. The dance itself crafted a new symbolic tool for interpreting and being involved in the story and for connecting that interpretation with surrounding children and adults.

Of equal importance were questions regarding how the teacher and her colleagues seemed to naturally view Isaac not as senselessly obstinate or in need of correction when, for instance, he refused to give up the book or when he started dancing, but rather as a child motivated to construct meaning within novel situations in an imaginative fashion. The adults engaged Isaac as a fully competent child—a literate citizen—with views, opinions, desires, and stories to tell. That his spoken voice was difficult to decipher or that he had trisomy 21 did not diminish the teachers' sense of Isaac's motivation or complex symbolic presence.

Isaac's literacy did not occur in a vacuum. First at home and then at school, he was surrounded by other active citizens of the inclusive early childhood literate community. For instance, I was fascinated by the group of boys in the classroom who were on the carpet building roads out of wooden blocks. They were in fact authoring complex narratives through sophisticated sign systems. They had collectively decided that the form of wooden blocks in organized patterns captured the meaning of "road" to the degree required for their stories to unfold. Thus, the blocks became part of a sign system reflecting, at least momentarily, essential characteristics of a road—relatively straight, narrow, flat expanses that could be connected in stretches. Certainly the blocks did not capture all of what a road is; instead, they served the children as an agreed-on metaphor—*this is as if it's a road*. The capacity to translate meaning into metaphoric signs is also the essence of turning stories and experiences into lettered representations using the social tool of the alphabet.

In addition to the peer narratives woven through the block play on the carpet, I was also struck by Isaac's exposure to his new friends' discussion that flowed from the reading of *Where the Wild Things Are*. Isaac Johansson had previously been relegated to a segregated classroom not only absent of children's literature, but also absent of children discussing their connections to such literature. Suddenly Isaac had become a part of a setting where a girl sitting in circle time might rely on her experiences to chastise the storybook character Max for running with a fork, and the boy sitting next to her might admit to being sent to his room, as Max was, for some unnamed crime. In this setting, Isaac experienced potential paths of connection between one's own story and the stories of others. Indeed, he learned that other children also were sent to their rooms by frustrated parents!

ESTABLISHED CONSTRUCTIONS OF LITERACY

My formulation of the triadic literate profile and the early childhood literate community contrasts with other established models of young children's literacy. These contesting frameworks indicate that no single, absolute, all-encompassing, or agreed-on definition of early literacy exists. Indeed, although the lead or predominant discourse of the moment always takes on the appearance of objective or scientific truth, in actuality the meaning of the term *literacy* and the inferences cast by the phrase *literate citizen* shift across time and place. For instance, during the 19th century a distinction of literate citizenship was made between those who could and could not sign their own names, which was a skill that fewer than half of the adult population of even the most industrialized Western European countries (those that relied most heavily on alphabetic text) possessed at the time (Fernandez, 2001; Resnick & Resnick, 1977).

Old documents found at the Mennonite Heritage Museum in the southern Minnesota town of Mountain Lake demonstrate that into the 20th century in the United States many of my Mennonite ancestors had to place an X where a name was required. How could these skilled farmers, parents, builders, craftspeople, and artisans (most often rolled into one) have been unable to perform this seemingly basic literate act expected today of 5-year-old children? The answer, of course, lies in the social nature of literacy. What was thought to be so objectively real just a century ago now seems so objectionably bizarre and unreal. The seemingly natural reality of whole classes of people living in an illiterate state was, in fact, an entirely unnecessary and unnatural social creation that was then reified, or made concrete and actual, through a myriad of collective informal and formal social circumstances (e.g., by denying schooling in favor of labor).

The shifting sensibilities regarding the nature of literacy is certainly apparent in the relatively recent, contrasting discourses of young children's literacy development already mentioned. The model of emergent literacy, for instance, still rightly commands attention in its developmental explanation of young children's growth as readers and writers (Razfar & Gutierrez, 2003). Drawing largely on a Piagetian sense of the child and his or her language unfolding through a general sequence of naturally occurring stages, emergent literacy theorists postulate that capacities for reading and writing begin at birth (Landry & Smith, 2006). Infants, toddlers, and preschoolers are said to actively craft increasingly sophisticated constructs related to written text along particular natural, stable, universal trajectories of development if provided with rich language environments. The teacher's role is to create a developmentally appropriate, child-centered environment within which the child's natural proclivities might unfold (Zill & Resnick, 2006).

Whereas emergent literacy retains more than a foothold, the *basic skills–phonics* model currently dominates policy debates regarding young children's initial literacy development. Within this paradigmatic framework, written language is not intrinsic to the child, as spoken language is thought to be, but it is considered a relatively recent (in evolutionary time) and contrived cultural creation. Literacy is considered a point reached along a trajectory of sequenced, mechanized skills adhering to four component areas. Each of these components requires that the learning process be composed of direct instruction and drill.

The first component area is referred to as phonemic awareness. It is both the conscious awareness on the part of young children that words are made up of a variety of sound units or phonemes *and* the skills involved in breaking words into these component sound bits. Phonemic awareness is divided into the following main subconstructs (Wagner & Torgeson, 1987; Whitehurst & Lonigan, 2001):

1. Phonological sensitivity (i.e., the ability to detect and manipulate the sound structure of oral language)

2. Phonological memory (i.e., the ability to orally recall verbally presented material)

3. Phonological naming ability (i.e., the time taken [efficiency] in naming visually presented material)

4. Decoding ability (e.g., the ability to sound out words, which, it is argued, is a higher order subskill built on the other phonological processing skills listed)

The second component area within the basic skills–phonics approach is commonly referred to as the alphabetic principle. It is a general description of knowledge about the alphabet, including understanding that phonemes can be orthographically represented in the form of letters and letter combinations (called *graphemes*). The third component area, oral language, is associated with vocabulary development and correct English usage. A fourth component that may be included in descriptions of an early childhood basic skills approach to literacy is orthography or spelling and the rules associated with spelling (e.g., Adams, 1990, 2001; Adams, Foorman, Lundberg, & Beeler, 1998; McGuiness, 1997). The literate citizen, according to this framework, is ultimately one who has, through formal direct instruction and drill, mastered and combined sets of phonemic and graphemic subskills in linear fashion (Adams et al., 1998).

Of the four component areas focused on in the basic skills–phonics approach, the first, phonemic awareness, is considered fundamental to any and all further early, as well as middle and later, literacy skills. Phonemic awareness becomes the base rungs of what might be described as a ladder to literacy. Any further ascension is considered impossible if subskills are not mastered. Therefore, literacy is brought into the preschool in the form of phonemic awareness drills. Marilyn Adams (2001), the central proponent of current phonics, described deciphering phonemes before understanding text as learning to walk before running. It is an unfortunate, yet revealing, metaphor because many children do not learn to walk but still are successful at navigating the community. Perhaps in navigating the literate community there might also be varying or even multiple routes to citizenship?

Omitted from the basic skills–phonics approach to early literacy is focus on young children's narratives and multiple sign systems for capturing, fixing, and interpreting or conveying narratives. Meaning making is considered a later skill for older students. This lack of narrative interest is seen, for instance, in the ubiquitous literacy assessment test *Dynamic Indicators of Basic Early Literacy Skills* (DIBELS; Good & Kaminski, 2002), which is now linked to numerous state efforts to meet phonics benchmarks associated with federal education policy mandates. DIBELS materials state that the *big ideas* of preschool literacy are limited to phonological awareness and the alphabetic principle. In preschool, DIBELS's focus is placed on *initial sound fluency* (e.g., "Which word starts with the sound /t/?") and *word use fluency* (i.e., children must decide if a word is used correctly in a particular sentence).

The term *fluency* equates with speed. All DIBELS subtests are administered in 1 minute and require a teacher to hold a stopwatch, allowing just seconds for each response before moving to the next question. Not keeping up is equivalent to failure. In kindergarten, *letter naming fluency, phoneme segmentation fluency,* and *nonsense word fluency* are added to the literacy skills. Understanding and meaning (referred to in DIBELS lexicon as *retell fluency*) are not addressed until first grade.

A focus in preschool on direct instruction and drill related to phonemic awareness has come to dominate education policy in the United States. The federal Elementary and Secondary Education Act of 1965 (PL 89-10), renamed the No Child Left Behind Act of 2001 (NCLB; PL 107-110), emphasizes phonemic awareness and approved phonics programs as the singular beginning point of reading for preschool students. In Subpart II of NCLB, Congress stated that resources would be restricted to

> Literacy activities based on scientifically based reading research that supports the age-appropriate development of: (A) recognition leading to automatic recognition of letters of the alphabet; (B) knowledge of letter sounds, [and] the blending of sounds...[and] (C) an understanding that written language is composed of phonemes and letters each representing one or more speech sounds that in combination make up syllables, words, and sentences. (Part B, Subpart 2.a)

In 2003, the U.S. Department of Education personnel instructed the school districts of New York City, San Diego, and Boston to change reading and language arts programs or risk losing all Reading First funds associated with NCLB (Herszenhorn, 2004). The urban districts had been using *balanced* literacy curricula in the kindergarten and primary grades that embraced components other than just phonemic awareness and that made use of literature as opposed to programmed phonemic workbooks. Chancellor of the New York City Schools, Joel Klein, responded to the federal threat by pointing out that children in all three of the districts were making better assessed progress than were children in cities using phonics programs mandated by the U.S. Department of Education.

Chancellor Klein noted that the forced switch in curricula was "being done in the name of science, and the question is: Where's the science?" (Herszenhorn, 2004, p. F1). The question proved prophetic as just 2 years later the Department of Education's Inspector General (Office of the Inspector General, U.S. Department of Education, 2006) issued a scathing report on Reading First and other NCLB programs. The report documented how department officials deliberately bent the law to favor certain programs of self-interest and discouraged others with no regard given to research-based evidence on effectiveness. Nonetheless, New York acquiesced to federal pressure rather than risk losing vital monies. Goodman has pointed out that

Under NCLB state authorities are told which materials, which tests, and which methods their teachers may use. This year's first graders are more likely to spend much of their school day on phonics exercises and preparations for tests on reading skills with little time for reading stories and children's books. Writing instruction is likely to be spelling, handwriting, and grammar exercises with little time for writing stories. (2004, p. 4)

NCLB is actually the culmination of a federal movement to control the meaning of, and approaches toward, literacy going back decades. In 1981, President Reagan's Education Secretary, T.H. Bell, convened the National Commission on Excellence in Education (NCEE) made up of business leaders, college presidents, professors from a variety of fields, school board members, and school administrators. Two years later, the commission published its widely read open letter to the American people entitled *A Nation at Risk: The Imperative for Educational Reform* (NCEE, 1983) in which it decried the "rising tide of mediocrity" (p. A.1) in U.S. schools. The commission recommended a curricula shift toward what it referred to as "the new basics" (p. B.1) and argued for the expanded use of "a nationwide system of State and local standardized tests" (p. B.3).

Publication of *A Nation at Risk* was quickly followed by the government-sponsored *Becoming a Nation of Readers: The Report of the Commission on Reading* (Commission on Reading, 1985). This second report famously began "Reading is a basic life skill. It is a cornerstone for a child's success in school and, indeed, throughout life" (p. 1). The commission emphasized reading as the result of "techniques, tools, and testing" (p. vi) and suggested that direct "formal, structured, and intensive" (p. 29) phonics instruction should begin in preschool and largely displace traditional child-centered curricula orientations.

This new emphasis was solidified as the singular beginning point to literacy with the 1990 publication of Adams's government-sponsored report to Congress entitled *Beginning to Read: Thinking and Learning About Print*. Adams (1990) argued that the "cognitive energy and resources upon which skillful [reading] comprehension begins" required prior word recognition skills that are "rapid, effortless, and automatic" (p. 5). She identified instruction in phonics as the prelude to future comprehension. Education legislation and congressional reports throughout the 1990s emphasized phonics as the singular evidence-based and scientific-based approach to promoting literacy in early childhood (e.g., Goals 2000: Educate America Act of 1994, PL 103-227; Reading Excellence Act of 1998, PL 105-277). The National Reading Panel Report of 2000 (National Institute of Child Health and Human Development, 2000) was subtitled *An Evidence-Based Assessment of the Scientific Research Literature for Reading Instruction*.

Within the basic skills–phonics orientation, Adams described the reading process as follows:

a) A child encounters a written word (e.g., CAT), b) is able to ortho-graphically process that word (i.e., break it efficiently into its component graphemes or written parts), c) then cortically associates the recognized word with its corresponding speech sound (e.g., "Cat," spoken) *and* d) associate it with an objective semantic representation (e.g., a mind's por-trait of a generic cat), and finally e) interpret and understand the word within the context in which it is encountered such as in a story about a cat. (2001, pp. 70, 71)

Adams's description of the contextual understanding of a text as the final literate act preceded by an extensive sequence of skills inadvertently serves as a metaphor of any child's presumed global path into literacy. Shannon (1995) critically noted that within such a framework, no instructional consideration is given to the back-grounds or narratives (natured or nurtured) with which children enter preschool. He noted that in the earliest years of schooling, instruction begins with drills on phonemic segmentation and specific letter-recognition skills. As students achieve mastery, these skills are then followed by

The teaching of how to recognize and draw other letters, to recognize the sounds associated with letters, to blend those letter sounds to syllables and words, to place those words in grammatical phrases and sentences, to combine those sentences into paragraphs, and finally to arrange and interpret paragraphs into stories, essays, and the like. This additive process would be followed for both reading and writing and would ensure that all students would receive the same skills if they can work their way through the sequence *from letters to meaning* in a timely fashion. This approach is designed so that the school "products" will have stan-dard equipment, if they make it all the way to the end of the assembly line. (Shannon, 1995, p. 42, emphasis added)

The literate construction of meaning and understanding is reserved only for those children who have survived the early skill-and-drill programmed efforts. The metaphor of a singular ladder to literacy (or, in Shannon's [1995] words, an *assembly line*) with its initial de-emphasis on meaning and understanding appears to work for many students, but for those students who struggle with the academic cur-riculum in school, the configuration of the ladder to literacy goes fun-damentally unchallenged. The belief is that literacy is composed of the sum of its mastered parts (subskills). When these subskills are further reduced into sub-subskills, they are easier to directly drill (on the part of a professional instructor) and master (on the part of children whose struggles in school are considered to be specifically centered around learning to read).

PERCEPTIONS OF LITERACY FOR YOUNG CHILDREN WITH SIGNIFICANT DEVELOPMENTAL DISABILITIES

Except for the efforts of relatively few researchers, young children with significant developmental disabilities, including presumed cognitive delays, are largely absent from current policy discussions on early literacy. For these young children, Isaac being one, mastery of basic skills associated with phonics is commonly considered to be impossible (APA, 2004). In the mid-1990s, one decade after the *Becoming a Nation of Readers* (Commission on Reading, 1985) report decreed the fundamental importance of early literacy, Erickson and Koppenhaver (1995) lamented, "It's not easy trying to learn to read and write if you're a child with severe disabilities in U.S. public schools today" (p. 676). They explained,

> Your preschool teachers are unlikely to be aware of emergent literacy research or to include written language activities in your early intervention programs. Many of the teachers you encounter across your public school career do not view you as capable of learning to read and write and consequently provide you with few opportunities to learn written language. (1995, p. 676)

In the years since, children with significant developmental disabilities continue to be denied access to rich literacy opportunities (Kliewer & Biklen, 2001; Mirenda, 2003). Mirenda (2003) noted that young children with significant developmental disabilities are "often seen as 'too cognitively impaired' or 'not ready for' instruction in [literacy]" (p. 271).

A doctrinaire response to the majority of preschool children with significant developmental disabilities, one experienced briefly by Isaac, is for educators to steer them into education tracts of strict segregation. According to 2006 data provided by the U.S. Department of Education to Congress, less than one in three children age 3–5 years with a disability label are provided with inclusive early childhood placements (U.S. Department of Education, 2006). Access to general education opportunities is highly restricted, and literacy programs are commonly absent or are unrecognizable (Erickson & Koppenhaver, 1995; Mirenda, 2003).

Classrooms segregated for children with moderate to severe disabilities commonly have no child-oriented books or pretend play opportunities. This is based on the presumption that such opportunities lack function in the lives of children with disabilities (Kliewer, Fitzgerald, & Raschke, 2001; Kliewer & Landis, 1999; Mirenda, 2003). In a previous study, a colleague and I identified a particularly stark theme regarding literacy and segregated special education: The literate participation of many children with significant disabilities in segregated settings was commonly limited to extremely brief, adult-designed expressions of bodily needs. A child with limited spoken language might, for example, have a communication board with BATHROOM and EAT symbolized but little else. The expectation was that a child with significant disabilities had nothing to say beyond those few expressions of bodily function. The resulting lack of literacy is then blamed on what are considered to be the children's intrinsic impairments rather than recognized as a manifestation of the stagnant settings in which children have been placed.

In contrast to disability doctrine, however, my own research in conjunction with the work of certain others (e.g., Katims, 2000; Kluth & Chandler-Olcott, 2008; Koppenhaver & Erickson, 2003) has demonstrated that young children with significant developmental disabilities, including those with intellectual impairments, are able to develop sophisticated literacy skills beginning in the earliest years of schooling. In several ethnographies of literacy I have conducted with various colleagues, it became apparent that this realization arose in inclusive early childhood environments where the surrounding adults, both parents and teachers, held both a local understanding of children with disabilities and challenged the singular ladder to literacy theory so deeply ensconced in our professional discourse.

Emphasizing and supporting *all* children's motivated drive to make meaning, craft narratives, and engage multiple sign systems allowed those traditionally excluded young children to find citizenship in the dynamic literate community. For instance, in relation to young children with trisomy 21, I observed developing sophistication with signs and symbols in settings where

> Teachers rejected the definition of reading as an end-element to a sequence of isolated subskills requiring student conformity [but instead] defined literacy as an evolving, symbolic dimension intrinsic to each strand of the web of shifting relationships that made up the classroom community. Children engaged symbolic tools, at varying levels of effectiveness, as they constructed understanding through constant negotiation and renegotiation of relationships with peers, adults, and materials. (Kliewer, 1998a, p. 172)

In a separate ethnography conducted in inclusive classrooms involving several young children with presumed severe intellectual disabilities who were demonstrating literacy skills, my colleague David Landis and I concluded that for our participating teachers

> A child's literacy development was not seen as a purely intrinsic metamorphosis: the nonreader unfolding into the reader along some inflexible path of a priori sequenced stages or skills. Rather, reading was understood to be a social and cultural practice, one in which the child was guided into the surrounding literate milieu complete with expectations, thoughtful activities, useful resources, effective teaching, and others engaged in culturally valued literacy practices. As children assumed the role of reader, their capacities became more obvious which in turn supported an enhanced recognition of their reading abilities and potential. (Kliewer & Landis, 1999, p. 97)

In this study, Landis and I first promulgated the idea of local understanding as central to literacy development for children with significant developmental disabilities. We noted that

> Local understanding encompassed assumptions that originated not in a priori, universal laws of disability incompetence or rigid literacy-learning sequences, but in the teacher's relationship with an actual child surrounded by the immediate instructional context.... Local understanding emphasized practices derived from questioning how the student might best be supported in her achievement toward what is always a professionally indeterminable literate potential. (Kliewer & Landis, 1999, pp. 89–90)

In another ethnography focused on inclusive education and literacy development in children with significant disabilities (Kliewer & Biklen, 2001), we directly observed teachers bypassing various obstacles to printed language opportunities. Convention holds that basic skill mastery is itself predicated on attainment of some particular cognitive level. Thus, children with significant disabilities are commonly found stalled at a preliteracy, subliteracy, or *readiness* stage while proof of necessary intellect is demanded—an exceedingly difficult requirement to fulfill when access to literate symbols for the expression of one's intellect is profoundly restricted.

In contrast to convention, however, the teachers participating in this ethnography recognized that the social engagement of children in meaningful interactions with one another and with adults actually fostered and facilitated the development of what we commonly consider to be internalized symbolic capacities (i.e., those capacities associated with language, literacy, and symbols that allow us to interact meaningfully). In essence, the teachers we studied turned convention upside down. Rather than waiting for signs of development prior to engagement within situations demanding symbolic skills, the teachers placed children, regardless of supposed cognitive level, in such social situations. With thoughtful support, this allowed children to demonstrate literate skills and show what we commonly refer to as cognitive development.

A child named Rebecca is an example of this ethnography in action (Kliewer & Biklen, 2001). Rebecca was a new student to the district and her inclusive fourth-grade classroom. She was presumed to have severe intellectual disabilities. Biklen and I reported that the teaching team agreed that its initial responsibility was, as one teacher expressed, "to make [Rebecca] a part of this [classroom] community" (2001, p. 6).

Under the guidance of adults, Rebecca's peers brainstormed ways to include her socially. One clique of girls came up with the idea that Rebecca should not be left out of their surreptitious note passing. The teaching team pointed out that the note passing was really Rebecca's first foray into symbolic, peer-guided communication. By the middle of the school year, with adult support, Rebecca was sending notes to her friends that she had "written" from symbols, pictures, and words provided—a symbolic capacity that had, according to her file, been considered well beyond her capabilities. Her teachers suggested that Rebecca's literate development occurred precisely because she was placed in social contexts where human connection through symbols was demanded. In this study, Biklen and I described the typically developing peers as demonstrating a local understanding of Rebecca through which they were able to "see in idiosyncratic behavior demonstrations of understanding that are otherwise dismissed or disregarded by more distant observers" (Kliewer & Biklen, 2001, p. 4).

Finally, in a literacy ethnography conducted with several colleagues in numerous inclusive early childhood classrooms, we uncovered the powerful literate affect of teachers supporting the participation of young children with significant developmental disabilities in what we termed the *imaginative life* of the classroom. We noted that

> In the classrooms involved in this study, teachers actively sought to support students with significant disabilities alongside their nondisabled peers in the full range of narrative forms comprising the early childhood literate community. Thus, the participating teachers demonstrated a fundamental belief in the capacity of children with significant developmental disabilities to engage in narratives of transcendence in which the imagination and interests of young children prodded their focus from the here-and-now and shifted it to the abstractions of play and stories. (Kliewer et al., 2004, p. 383)

Particularly important findings from the four studies described here include 1) understanding literacy as a social tool for the construction of meaning on the part of all children (with or without disabilities), 2) the importance of immersing children into the literate community (rather than segregating them from it) with teachers as thoughtful guides, 3) supporting children's use of sign and symbol systems rather than stalling the child in a perpetual presymbol stage, and 4) seeing the imaginative potential of all children (with or without disabilities).

These dimensions are fundamental to the three guiding principles of local understanding (which are discussed in depth in the following chapters).

1. A deeply ensconced vision of the child's rightful participation, or full citizenship, in valued communities, including the literate community of inclusive early childhood educational environments

2. The determination and actuality of crafting inclusive literate communities that foster all children's active participation

3. The importance of collaboration among educational professionals and the child's family to achieve the first two principles

Chapter 3

"We Going a Space"

Cardboard Boxes, Rockets, and the
Child's Literate Construction of Meaning

The conceptual framework of *local understanding* arose from my investigations of inclusive early childhood programs and the literate development occurring therein for children labeled with significant developmental disabilities. Local understanding is both a moral stance and an organizational dialogue around the competence of children in a particular setting. It is a situated, dual-pronged conversation of human capacity. That is, in the arena of literacy, teachers, various education personnel, and families envision, without qualifiers, the child's literate citizenship or right to full participation in the surrounding literate community. Also, they strive to craft that community as a responsive, actualizing social context of meaningful relationships, resources, and symbolic materials through which the child's active citizenship might be fostered and realized. As the child's literate sophistication extends and deepens, so, too, does the complexity of the context in relation to the child.

CHILDREN'S LITERATE CITIZENSHIP
FORMED FROM THE TRIADIC LITERATE PROFILE

Within early childhood programs that are organized on local understanding, the literate community refers to the valued, democratic connectedness that is fostered as children symbolically construct representational meaning of their surrounding world. In general, the symbols and sign systems used are those associated with the representational rather than communicative edge of the early childhood expressive continuum described in Chapter 2. Literate citizenship within the community is a dynamic manifestation of a child's literate profile that interactively includes the following:

1. The visual, orthographic, and tactile symbol and sign systems within which narratives are caught (i.e., given form and shape), fixed (i.e., given a relative degree of stability), and interpreted (i.e., made sense of) or conveyed (i.e., expressed)

2. The narratives (e.g., stories) created by children through which meaning is constructed

3. A child's symbolic presence (i.e., the collaborative drive and potential to imagine and make sense of the surrounding world)

Conventional interest in literacy has primarily focused on interactions (or, in the case of younger children, preinteractions) with alphabetic text and the precursor subskills contained therein. Even when a research focus is constrained to this conventional arena, ferocious debate ensues. Is literacy a set of skills (Kulleseid & Strickland, 1989), a core area of accumulated knowledge (Bianculli, 1992), or a perspective on the world (Potter, 2004)? Here I maintain a strong interest in alphabetic text and the literate growth of young children with significant developmental disabilities, but, as noted, I have also realized through my research that this focus must expand as the complexities of early literacy deepen in relation to all children, with or without disabilities.

This chapter provides an explanatory introduction to the composition of the young child's literate profile, which is further expanded on in Chapter 4. Following this introduction are a series of data vignettes from 2 days of observation in a single classroom. Woven through this description are commentary and interpretation designed to highlight, in a version of real time, glimpses of local understanding, the triadic literate profile, and the literate community. The remainder of the chapter retrieves aspects of this data along with data presented in the first two chapters and from other observations to extend the discussion of literacy development in young children with significant developmental disabilities.

Visual, Orthographic, and Tactile Symbol and Sign Systems

Regarding the three constructs of the young child's literate profile, children's motivated efforts with multiple visual, orthographic, or tactile symbol and sign systems was the first to emerge in my qualitative data.

This was primarily due to my initial ideology equating all of literacy to children's engagement with alphabetic text—an orthographic sign system. I entered the field of inclusive preschools and kindergartens intent on observing how written language as a singular entity was made available to, or denied, young children with disabilities. I quickly realized that written language was not unidimensional or a monolith; rather, it swirled around the children from computer screens, to jotted notes, to recipes, to picture books, to competing fonts, to print and cursive and upper and lower cases in numerous integrated formats, styles, functions, spatial arrangements, and modalities.

Furthermore, systematic observations led me to understand that children's interactions with alphabetic language made up just one slice of their efforts to create and engage a myriad of other visual or tactile symbol and sign systems to capture, fix, and interpret or convey meaning. As described in Chapter 2, I retained a strong interest in children's alphabetic written language efforts; however, I quickly realized that to understand the literate citizenship of any child required exploring the breadth of their engagement with ranges of sign systems.

The terms *sign* (used to this point interchangeably with the word *symbol*) and *sign system* are actually technical terms defined and used by researchers and theorists who study language from a *social semiotic perspective*. Within this framework, language is a system of signs. Spoken and written language constitutes different sign systems. Music is a system of signs. Photos, paintings, and even doodles all have cultural histories and contexts and make use of an array of sign systems. Clothing is a sign system that expresses varying narratives regarding our (momentary and extended) sense of personal display (e.g., formal, casual, preppy, hippy, hip-hop). Children's play is built on complex sign systems.

Certain visual, orthographic, or tactile sign systems have a degree of permanence. One example of this is the drawing of several figures (with heads, no torsos, and very long stick legs) produced by Andrew, a 4-year-old student without disabilities in an inclusive preschool. The picture was Andrew's representational effort to depict four family members at his brother's birthday party. The figures were arranged around a blue blob, and several were floating. Also included in the drawing were somewhat isolated, identifiable alphabetic letters and unidentifiable squiggles that looked as though they were meant to be letters. Andrew, emerging from his representational effort to communicate his thoughts, explained the blue blob to be a cake and the letters and squiggles (letter approximations) to represent the names of the people in the picture. In its relative permanence, this particular drawing was hung on the wall of the classroom with a teacher-written caption, "Andrew's brother's birthday party!" Other sign systems were more fleeting but no less symbolic or powerful. Isaac's dance to the storybook *Where the Wild Things Are* (see Chapter 1) is also an example.

Narratives

I observed children with support from adults who would link and interchange sign systems in the development and interpretation of stories, or what I came to refer to as *narratives*, which are the medial dimension of the literate profile. Indeed, through careful observation I came to realize that children were constantly in the process of creating narratives in their ongoing efforts to make sense of the surrounding world. *Narrative* is a succinct term meant to capture the symbolic embodiment (from stable to ethereal) of experience, autobiography, biography, ideas, thoughts, concerns, interests, desires, emotions, visions, fantasies, and stories.

Containment within some sort of textual or symbolic structure allows a narrative to be told, made sense of, understood, retold, altered, and so forth such that a symbolic connectedness (a literate community) is crafted in the classroom. Andrew's picture of the birthday party helped tell the tale of the party. Isaac's dance aided in the interpretation of Max's rumpus dance. Isaac demonstrated perhaps a counterintuitive sense of construction in that listening to a story read is also an act of narrative creation, not just decoding or interpretation, as children wrench and spin meaning from the words of another. The term *narrative* is arguably less constrained in its cultural definitions than is *story* and so better captures the breadth and complexities of young children's meaning making.

Visual, orthographic, and tactile sign systems, in interaction with spoken language, were born of the collective need to express narratives. I was able to *see* the shape of narratives through the integrated sign systems children collectively churned and mixed together. For instance, as Andrew chose a blue marker and began to draw, he created a particular narrative structure balancing between representation and communication. "This is the blue cake. My mom always makes his cakes blue." Thus, he combined the sign system of spoken language with the visual and orthographic sign systems embodied in drawn, representational figures and hovering alphabetic letters.

Symbolic Presence

As sign systems were born of narratives, narratives, in turn, were born of and gave shape to children's symbolic presence—their drive and potential to collaboratively and imaginatively construct meaning and make symbolic sense of the surrounding world. Fundamental to Andrew's birthday party narrative and its expressive form(s) was a drive to make sense of experience and then use that meaning to connect with others. The picture he created to extend and document the narrative of the birthday was obviously not a mirror reflection of reality, but was how Andrew *imagined* the party to be. Through documenting narratives, I encountered and began to realize the full power of children's motivation to communally relate, order, organize, investigate, extend on, overturn, and leap from experience in a manner that connects with others.

INTERRELATIONSHIP OF THE CONSTRUCTS OF THE YOUNG CHILD'S LITERATE PROFILE

The symbolic presence serves, in a sense, as the primordial origin of any child's literacy. It inspires the shape of the narrative that inspires the forms of sign systems. In a somewhat cyclic turn, the form of signs accessible to the child flow back to have an impact on the shape of the narrative that influenced the symbolic presence. Whether the child is producing an original text (e.g., drawing a picture of a birthday party) or consuming a text crafted by another (e.g., listening to a storybook), the triadic model remains. In both instances the child is motivated through his or her symbolic presence to construct meaning and does so by crafting a narrative that is meant to connect with others or that meaningfully links with the text of others (whatever their form).

Of course, experience (and lack of it), opportunities opened (and shut), and materials made (and not made) available act to both liberate and set limits on the range of sign systems created and enacted by children. In turn, this has an impact on how narratives might be considered and structured, which affects the dynamics of the child's symbolic presence. Although I do see literacy as primarily originating in the symbolic presence, structured through narrative and conveyed in visual, orthographic, or tactile symbol or sign, the flow of literacy is never entirely a unidirectional enterprise. Rather, the triadic components are intertwined with each in the array affecting and being affected by the other. The following scenario is from an observation occurring during a 2-day period in a classroom actively demonstrating local understanding and children's citizenship in the inclusive early childhood literate community.

THE BETHEL ROCKET

Judith Perry's voice rose above those of her 17 students, who were 4 years old or just turning 5 and were scattered throughout the classroom at the Bethel Nursery School. "You tell me what you need to make it work," the co-lead teacher was saying to Jared and Duane, two students intent on stabilizing the construction of a cardboard box rocket ship near the center of the expansive room in the basement of the Bethel Church. The rocket was one of several projects related to the current theme of the solar system. A number of child-oriented books on outer space lined shelves, and orb-shaped models of child-created pâpier mâché planets splotched with paint hung from the ceiling.

The Bethel teachers had chosen the solar system as the 2-week theme of the class based largely on the expressed interest of several children. As such, local understanding was apparent in that children's motivations and interests were seriously considered when designing curricula. In an interview, Ms. Perry noted, "Well, we had a bunch of students going crazy over anything to do with moons and planets and UFOs. Jeremy [a student] brought in this book [*Noah and the Space Ark*, Cecil, 1998] and [co-teacher] Petra [Solodett] and I, we're like, 'Well, this was pretty happening last year so maybe we should do it again but expand.'"

Ms. Perry was pointing out that children's symbolic presence and their drive to make meaning is a collaborative enterprise exploding forth from children and adults in action together. Furthermore, as a manifestation of their symbolic presence, at least certain children expressed a motivation to understand not just earthly realms but also distant worlds.

The related books brought in by children and adults, some fact based and some fictional, contained stories made up of alphabetic-based text, which is a particular sign system, in combination with either picture-based signs or photo-based signs. Whether these books were read to the students or enjoyed apart from adults, the children were engaged in acts not just of narrative reproduction, consumption, digestion, or acquisition, but of actual narrative production. Children's interpretations of the language or pictures of a book are acts of creation in which they bring their own life stories, histories, and experiences (what Piaget referred to as *schema*) into a new narrative form of connection. Certainly the intentions of the book's author and illustrator constrain and lend form to how the story unfolds, but the child in interaction with any other children involved also profoundly influences the ultimate shape of the end story.

Numerous child-initiated narratives were inspired by the cardboard box that had been transformed earlier into a rocket. As a rocket, the box was a sign or symbol constructed out of numerous other signs. For instance, Popsicle sticks were stuck through slots to form representations of levers that could assist astronauts with liftoff and flight. String attached to a paper cup on the interior served as a radio microphone. In addition, the pâpier-mâché planets that hung from the ceiling were symbols that aided children in telling various solar system narratives, some of which were reflective of space facts. Four-year-old Julian, for example, painted red figures on one of the planets to represent what he termed *aliens*, thus opening an interesting narrative.

Julian's friend, Marley, a 4-year-old considered to have significant developmental disabilities, laid newspaper strips covered in watery glue over a balloon. A teacher said, "Now when this dries we'll paint our planet."

Marley protested, "Ba-oon," seemingly arguing from a literal stance over what he had just created.

Although some may attribute Marley's view of what had been created to his disability, a number of children without disabilities also seemed to think that they were crafting a new kind of balloon to be hung from the ceiling. Believing that these were some new form of balloons despite repeated teacher explanations of their planetary representation appeared to make perfect sense to some of the children.

Alicia, a 5-year-old student, told her father one morning, "These are our balloons for the solar party."

A nearby student responded, "Them is planets!"

Alicia appeared completely unfazed by the intended correction. She was simply making sense of the symbols in her environment. Her father winked at the other student and responded to Alicia, "Very nice balloons."

The day prior to my observation of Jared and Duane being concerned with the stability of the cardboard rocket, I had watched another child, Starr, paint the words *Bethel Raket* (i.e., Bethel Rocket) along one side of the structure under the guidance of her friend Lori. Starr, clad in a floor-length smock, was a typically developing 4-year-old. Lori, 2 months shy of her fifth birthday, had cerebral palsy, which resulted in her use of a wheelchair and difficulty with speech. Previously, she was labeled as having cognitive delays, but her teachers at Bethel and her parents were skeptical of the diagnosis. Their local understanding of Lori allowed them to see capacity where developmental assessments had emphasized inability. Lori, along with Marley and Joey, was one of three children in the class with significant developmental disabilities.

To indicate which letter Starr was to paint, Lori reached out and touched a keyboard communication device, known as a *Dynavox*. An associate teacher, Margaret Lee, stabilized her in a sitting position out of her wheelchair on the floor. Lori touched the letter *B*. A computer-generated child's voice from the Dynavox intoned, "Beee." Ms. Lee repeated, "Beee," and Starr painted a line straight down, dipped her brush, and carefully painted one loop facing to the left of her original line. She dipped her brush again and painted a second loop above the first, which formed the semblance of a backward letter *B*. Starr smiled at her completed letter with a look of pride.

Lori's chin sunk toward her chest, but she arched her eyebrows and, over her glasses, watched Starr with intensity. She reached out to the device, uncurled her fingers, and touched the letter *E*. The robotic voice sounded, "Eee." Ms. Lee said, "Eee." Starr again painted a line straight down. This time without retrieving more paint, she quickly made three cross lines beginning at the bottom of the line. The first was longer than the middle, which was longer than the top cross line.

"Eee," said Starr.

Several minutes earlier, Ms. Lee had approached Starr and Lori, described by adults as best friends, to ask, "Girls, we need to name our rocket. Do you want to help?" Starr suggested it be named *Bethel Rocket*.

Ms. Lee looked at Lori, who at that point was supported in a standing-frame, a device with a platform and straps that held her up vertically, and asked, "Does that sound like a good name?" Lori made a sound from her throat and dropped her head in a nod indicative of consent.

Lori's close relationship with Starr was predicated on her full participation in the chaotic flow of the busy nursery school classroom. According to the tenets of local understanding, Lori's citizenship, and thus her competence to be a citizen, was assumed. As such, when it came time to construct the narrative of naming the rocket and then labeling it with paint, Ms. Lee did not hesitate to seek out Lori's symbolic capacities. Indeed, Lori's alphabetic abilities, well known to the teachers, were central to maintaining the child centeredness of the activity.

Lori's high-level ability to spell emerged over the course of several months as a result of her drive to communicate. Lori had entered the class with a very limited array of sounds and gestures that were imbued with meaning by those who knew her well. Teachers and the language therapist at Bethel immediately created sets of labeled symbols that Lori could gaze at or gesture toward to express a menu of needs. The language therapist began experimenting with various forms of assistive technology at the same time her teachers began to emphasize letters as constitutive of words. Lori took to both the technology and the written language instruction with intensity and focus. She was quickly spelling from memory. These important abilities flowed from her teachers' sense of her symbolic presence, her capacity to craft narratives, and her competence with sign systems.

Starr, a typically developing child, shared a strong interest in books with Lori, and as a result the two developed a deep relationship. Ms. Perry told me,

> Their friendship really started in the library [corner of the classroom]. They both were always there; Starr begging one of us to read to them.

Starr did not yet have Lori's ability to chain together letters into meaningful words; however, she was motivated to produce letters as indicated through her participation in naming the rocket. Her formation of the letters contained both elements of function (ultimately spelling out the dictated word) and form. These letters were not just functional subentities without stories; they stood alone as acts or forms of creation. She was every bit drawing the letters as much as she was writing them. They had, in a sense, lives of their own.

I continued to observe as Lori finished dictating the letters to the word *Bethel* in correct order while Starr crafted flourishing approximations and swooping semblances of their pictorial representations. At one point, Ms. Lee told Lori to wait with the next letter until Starr completed her current effort. Several other children moved in and out of the scene.

One boy said, "You drawing it wrong. It's supposed to go this way," while he waved his arm up and down. Starr's effort ran left to right, but the boy thought a rocket's letters should run from top to bottom, which is indicative of the importance children place on spatial arrangements in the representation of sign systems.

His phrase *drawing it* reflected my earlier point about Starr's acts of creation. That is, when children form letters they are in essence "drawing words." In addition, children this age most often "write pictures" in the sense that the drawings represent stories and narratives. For children with significant developmental disabilities who are affected physically, symbol formation is often constrained to keyboards or to prefabricated symbols. This certainly makes sense, but the element of creation is rendered less visible. Words are not drawn, and pictures are not written. (This is an important concept that will be further discussed in Chapter 5.)

Although *Bethel* was a familiar word visibly posted throughout the rooms of the church basement and invoked several times a day in formal and informal discussion (e.g., "Bethel kids, come to the table for snack"), *rocket* was not. Lori hesitated before beginning to spell rocket. Starr waited, poised with brush in hand.

"Rrrrocket," Ms. Lee said to Lori, emphasizing the beginning letter. "What letter makes the 'rrrrrr' sound?"

Lori reached out, uncurled her clenched fingers, and with her middle finger touched the R. The computer voice said, "R," and Ms. Lee said, "R, good. R, Starr." Starr painted a circle, dipped her brush, and added two sticks aimed down for her version of an R.

Ms. Lee said to Lori, "What letter comes next? Rrrraawwket."

Lori hesitated a moment, her body slumped slightly forward. She lifted her head and touched the letter A. The computer said, "A."

Ms. Lee said, "Do you want A? Are you choosing A?"

Ms. Lee's reaction was a fairly obvious cue that an incorrect choice had been made, but Lori smiled and made an affirmative sound that came from the back of the throat as she moved her torso forward.

Ms. Lee said, "Okay, Starr, A." Starr painted the A. In this way the small group completed, in highly collaborative fashion, the christening of the cardboard rocket. The final sign read *Bethel Raket*.

The inclusion of children with disabilities at Bethel Nursery School had begun 4 years prior to this observation of Lori and her peers. Originally, the mother of another child with cerebral palsy who lived in a neighborhood near Bethel had sought to place her daughter in a nearby preschool—the same one the child's older siblings had attended. Personnel at that preschool had refused the girl's admittance, saying she was "too disabled." Startled, the mother approached other early childhood centers in the immediate area only to have her daughter rejected again and again. Finally, she ended up at the door of Bethel.

The director of the nursery, Petra Solodett, who served as co-lead teacher with Ms. Perry, as well as financial manager, recalled telling the mother,

> ❝ We would love to have your child become part of our community. We don't have experience with children with severe disabilities, so we'll seek out some support. ❞

Ms. Solodett and Ms. Perry then made contact with the Shoshone School (described in Chapter 1), which was located in the same city. Shoshone had a far-reaching reputation for effective inclusion. From that initial plea for assistance, a partnership of shared resources and expertise began between Bethel and Shoshone.

The story of inclusion at Bethel demonstrated an intuitive sense on the part of the teachers regarding a child's rightful place in the general community of early childhood programs. A child's distinct or unique needs associated with disability did not result in the child's banishment or elimination from the setting but served as the genesis for problem solving from the framework of local understanding. The question aimed at the child (and her parents), "Do you really belong here?" was altered to "How do we support your belonging here?"

On the day following my observation of the painting of *Bethel Raket*, Starr and Lori were elsewhere, and the two boys, Jared and Duane, wanted to stabilize the nose cone, which was a second cardboard piece attached to the top of the rocket that now leaned precariously.

"You tell me," Ms. Perry said, "and we'll see if that works." Jared suggested duct tape in a tentative tone. "Maybe," Ms. Perry said. "See if we have any."

The symbolic motivation during this incident was one of engineering and mechanics that allowed the boys to understand and desire the valued role of rocket repair people. The narrative was basically the story of fixing a perceived flaw in the rocket.

A primary sign or symbol involved in the structuring of this narrative was the rocket itself. In transforming the cardboard box into a rocket, similar to the group of boys who created roads out of wooden blocks at the Shoshone School, the children had in fact created a metaphor, which is both a basic feature of literacy (the symbol representing the actual) and an important tool for furthering the power of visual, orthographic, or tactile sign systems. The box did not represent an entire rocket. Rather, it represented enough of the key features to be *like* a rocket. It was as if the box became a rocket.

In its original form, and even better now that it was decorated, the box contained enough critical features to take on a particular *rocketness*. Characteristics such as the interior suggesting snug containability, added gadgets representing a control panel, and the general form suggesting tubular mobility all coalesced to symbolize *rocket*. The child's transition from symbolizing a rocket using a box to spelling out R-A-K-E-T is (metaphorically) considered a, if not the only, primary story of children's literacy. (In Chapter 4, I will examine this symbolic traverse in depth.)

While Jared went off to look in a bin labeled "tape," Ms. Perry left the area, and Duane climbed through a round opening cut in the rocket. Duane was considered to have speech and language impairments, although his teachers described the condition as mild in nature relating generally to his articulation. He began shaking the box from the inside while making sounds mimicking those of a rocket blasting off. Joey watched Duane from the periphery of the play area. Joey, a tall boy with shining brown eyes and sandy hair, was 4 years and 9 months old. He had limited, highly repetitive speech. At age 3 years, his physician labeled him as having autism spectrum disorder in combination with significant cognitive delays. *Spectrum* indicates that in aggregate fashion people with this diagnosis function on a continuum ranging from severe to minimal disability. According to this convention, Joey fell toward the severe side.

Joey ran toward the shaking box, slapped at the door flap, then bounced backward on his tiptoes, letting out a high-pitched squeal that continued in a vibrato for several seconds. Even in the hectic nursery school classroom with children and adults moving in all sorts of directions, a classroom aide, Merry Schurta, was quick to notice Joey on the periphery of the play. She moved into the scene, reaching for Joey's hand, and gently tugged him toward the rocket. "You're going for a ride to the moon!" Ms. Schurta said.

Duane, inside the box, overheard Ms. Schurta's voice. He stuck his head out the flap and without hesitation and looking directly at Joey, said, "Joey, we going a space! You got to...[not understood] for Jared. We fix this rocket."

Duane's head snapped back into the rocket. Joey slapped at the box, giggled wildly, and ran around the structure. This time he did not exit the area. Ms. Schurta turned her attention elsewhere. Duane stepped out of the box and came at Joey in a slow walk with arms out as if he were moving through Jell-O.

"Robot," Duane said in a slow voice.

Joey stood still with a wide smile, and Duane's arms came down over him in a bear hug. With an arm around his shoulder, Duane steered Joey toward the rocket door. Once inside the rocket, Joey grabbed hold of a paper cup microphone hanging from a string stuck through the cardboard. Joey put the cup over his mouth and made squealing sounds. Duane nodded approvingly.

"Yeah," Duane said, "We gots ta radio the headquarters."

In this chain of interactions, local understanding emanated from Ms. Schurta's awareness of Joey's perimetric actions and the manner in which she imbued them with meaning. Joey was not treated as a child with severe autism behaving in random fashion but was considered first and foremost a citizen of the class with a symbolic presence motivated to connect with others and make sense of his surroundings. "You're going for a ride to the moon," Ms. Schurta said, lending a descriptive voice to the construction of narrative where admittedly an ambiguity existed.

Perhaps in her ascription, Ms. Schurta missed the mark. We have a limited sense of knowing what Joey is fully imagining, and some researchers question if a child with severe autism is imagining at all (APA, 2004). In the Bethel Nursery School, however, teachers viewed all children as able to imagine or as having a symbolic presence. For any young child, there is always difficulty knowing the full breadth of his or her imagination. For Joey, this was exasperated due to his struggles with conventional communication. Maybe he was not thinking about space flight at all. Maybe his intentions were to fly to Mars rather than the moon.

In a later discussion on this point, Ms. Solodett pointed out that while teachers do exert more influence over Joey's narratives than they do with most other children, "Joey definitely can tell us when we have it wrong!" She continued, "It wasn't that long ago that he used his little teeth clamping down on you to let you know." This comment alluded to the biting that he did as a form of protest earlier in the school year. "Now," Ms. Solodett said, "he just throws one hell of a tantrum." Joey's acceptance of Ms. Schurta's support near the rocket suggested to the teaching team that, within this example, the adult was on track in interpreting Joey.

Beyond Ms. Schurta's support for Joey, I was struck by his interaction with his peer, Duane. A tone of local understanding seemed to permeate the entire setting, not just the adults in the classroom. Duane was happy to see a friend enter the narrative and knew precisely how to further Joey's participation. Duane did not speak through a teacher to Joey but directly to his friend. Joey had general struggles moving from the periphery to the center of any activity without actual physical cues, pushes, and prods. Duane's playful approach to physically assisting Joey's entrance to the rocket was precisely what Joey required. Duane's actions demonstrated a real sensitivity toward Joey. Finally, when Joey reached for the microphone, which was itself a metaphoric sign, Duane's response indicated that he had no question that Joey was sustaining and furthering the narrative of space flight.

At the end of the school day, Ms. Perry was sitting with several children at a table. She was positioned immediately to the right of Joey and had a number of note cards laid out on which she had earlier written and pictorially symbolized the following words: *Bethel Rocket* (with a simple drawing of a rocket-shaped box), *cooking activity* (with a drawing of a pan), *outside play* (drawing of a sun), and *blocks* (drawing of three block figures). Ms. Perry read and pointed to each card. She asked Joey, "Which should I write home about?"

Ms. Perry placed a stabilizing hand on Joey's arm. He reached out and grabbed the card that read *Bethel Rocket*. Ms. Perry wrote in a notebook, "I played in the Bethel Rocket." She rifled through another set of well-worn cards with the names of classmates written on them. She laid out five and, without reading them, said, "Who should I say you played with?" With Ms. Perry's arm again on his, Joey picked up Duane's name. Ms. Perry wrote in the notebook, "I played with Duane."

Ms. Perry's co-construction of the note with Joey demonstrated the teaching team's sense of Joey's capacity to use signs and symbols in the construction of a reflective narrative, specifically a message to his parents describing important moments from his day. The note also, of course, demonstrated the teachers' local sense that Joey could reflect at all. Had they relied on distant, institutional interpretations of severe autism, Joey would not have been approached as a literate citizen. Indeed, he probably would have been in a segregated learning environment.

The practice of creating notes to be sent home was a teacher-guided daily ritual unique to the three children in the class with significant developmental disabilities. It was an active means of retaining a consistent connection with the children's families, two of whom had mothers who regularly wrote notes back to the teachers. Bethel teachers had developed methods whereby each of the children, Joey, Lori, and Marley, could participate in the authorship of the note.

Joey's capacity to recognize sight words, similar to his classmate Lori's ability to spell, actually demonstrated conventional literacy skills beyond the complexity level of most of his typically developing peers. As with Lori's skills, Joey's ability with print was originally recognized by teachers through efforts to foster his limited communication. The minimal physical or facilitated support teachers provided Joey's hand or arm when he reached out to make word choices reflected Joey's struggle to organize, initiate, and direct his voluntary movements apart from physical cues. This was the same general type of physical support he received from his friend Duane who helped him move into the cardboard box.

As Ms. Perry and Joey worked together, the children surrounding them engaged in a myriad of narratives using a range of visual, orthographic, or tactile sign systems. For instance, a student at the table snacked on Frito chips. When asked what he was eating, the student held up the chip bag and in exaggerated fashion enunciated, "Freee-toes," while he poked at the brand name with his index finger. He clearly felt the response to the question was disdainfully obvious.

Next to the churlish snacker sat Jared from the morning observation and another boy drawing war scenes using markers on a single sheet of large paper. The picture in conjunction with spoken narration and sound effects contained a rather violent storyline. Also at the table sat a girl flipping through a picture book. She went from front to back, but at times she flipped to a page she had already looked at, as though she needed to recheck something. At one point she did this and held the book up toward Ms. Perry saying, "The hippo has pajamas that are too little." She started laughing.

Ms. Perry laughed with her and said, "That kind of looks like me in my pajamas."

"JUST SHOOTING FOR THE STARS" AND OTHER CONCLUDING THOUGHTS

The theme of solar system took place at the Bethel Nursery School in late winter, approximately 6 months into the school year. The week prior to school beginning in late August, I had spent time with the teachers as they met and prepared for the coming year. At that point, Joey, Lori, and Marley, the three students considered to have significant developmental disabilities, were just abstractions to me. When asked if there were general goals for the coming literacy activities being discussed and organized, Ms. Perry responded, "Just shooting for the stars."

Ms. Solodett interjected,

> For every kid. We shoot for the stars for every one of these kids.

Her hand gestured toward a bulletin board on which hung every child's name.

Six months later, watching the students relish in space flight, planets, and aliens, I reminded Ms. Perry of her quote. "Is this what you meant?" I joked.

Ms. Perry laughed, but then pointed out, "Look how far we've come. Can you even believe it?"

Lori had begun the school year communicating primarily through a limited range of sounds. The teaching team never hesitated in its communal sense of Lori's symbolic presence. She was presumed to be a little girl with much to say. Initially she was provided picture symbols to assist in the construction of narratives, but she moved on to assistive technology and, when useful, actual spelling at a level well beyond the capacity of any of her peers.

During the first weeks of school, Joey had thrown intense tantrums and regularly bitten several of the adults in the room. As he began to develop relationships with other children, his biting became nonexistent. His communication, fostered out of the teachers' sense of his symbolic presence, incorporated the ability to read whole words.

Marley had gone from being largely untestable on developmental screenings in the beginning of the school year to scoring 12–14 months shy of his chronological age by the end of the year. Although this would still be interpreted as developmentally delayed, the growth was astounding.

At Bethel, as in my other participating inclusive early childhood education sites, shooting for the stars in the literate community originated on an absolute acceptance of the child's right to belong. Limited mobility or communication, severe aggression or tantrums, and low developmental assessment scores were not one-way tickets into a segregated oblivion absent of critical literacy opportunities. Rather, the child with significant developmental disabilities was recognized as inherently motivated to imagine, construct meaning, and develop a connectedness with peers, and he or she was supported in the crafting of narratives through a range of visual, orthographic, or tactile sign systems. In collaboration with local understanding, this made reaching the stars a very real possibility.

Chapter 4

" I See All My Kids as Readers! "

Symbolic Presence, Narrative Construction, and Literacy Signs

In the previous chapter, based on notes from 2 days of observation at the Bethel Nursery School, I offered several vignettes of children interacting with one another while working on a solar system theme. Some of the students were labeled with significant developmental disabilities. Others were considered typically developing. Highlighted were illustrations of local understanding and the constructs of the early childhood literate profile. The chapter would have been far slimmer had I approached the given data from a conventional early literacy approach.

The frameworks of emergent literacy, basic skills–phonics, or some ostensibly balanced approach are largely constrained to fairly rigid definitions of children's *meaningful engagement* with alphabetic text. Using the previous chapter as an example, such a locus might include the following:

1. Teacher oversight of appropriate reading materials and lettered activities for the exploration of the solar system theme

2. Lori, a child with disabilities, determinably typing out the semi-phonetic spelling of *Bethel Rocket* in interaction with a teacher

3. Lori's friend, Starr, painting letters as they were dictated with a teacher present

4.   Jared searching for duct tape in a bin labeled "tape"

5.   A teacher working with Joey to write a note home

In accordance with conventional models, early literacy is closely associated with children acquiring what is believed to be a stable system associated with alphabetic print that allows an author to systematically encode ideas and convey those ideas across time and space to an audience able to decode the text.

Debate might ensue among proponents of the contesting early childhood literacy models over the meaning of *meaningful engagement* and the manner in which children's skills develop (either from the inside out or the outside in); however, common ground is found in a deeply ensconced belief that language, including written language, preexists for the child as a stable, even mechanistic, array of alphabetic signs, sounds, and rules to which the child conforms with increasing sophistication as developmental stages (inside out) or educational levels (outside in) are met and mastered.

The literacy researcher and social semiotic theorist Gunther Kress (1997) challenged this ubiquitous sense of stability and mechanics that permeates formal theory and day-to-day notions of language by suggesting that children actively create and transform sign systems rather than repeat and conform to them. He explained, "We can continue to assume that language is a stable system, beyond the effect of individual influence, either for social reasons (the force of convention [i.e., basic skills–phonics models]) or for psychological reasons (the nature of the brain or mind [i.e., emergent literacy models])" (p. xvi). Kress continued,

> The social perspective legitimates teaching language as a system of rules which must be "acquired" in their proper form, for example, as standard forms of the language. It encourages "correctness," adherence to authoritative systems and does not raise the question of individual freedom of action other than within constraints of this system. Psychological considerations make it possible to see the purpose of teaching to be to aid learners in developing their innate, inherent potential "properly" or "fully." Neither of the two approaches envisages the possibility of productive, transformative action by an individual child or adult in relation to language or literacy. (1997, p. xvi)

Kress's counter to convention—that is, his image of the individual in action as transformative and as a producer and not mere reproducer of signs and literacy systems—captures core principles fulminating from my ethnographic and grounded theoretical explorations of the literate lives of young children with and without developmental disabilities.

Ultimately, whether written language systems are intrinsic and natural, extrinsic and arbitrary, or something not yet thought of, the point is moot. Young children immersed in rich language contexts (e.g., the inclusive preschool or kindergarten community) do not act, behave, or think as though their literacy is naturally emergent or, conversely, cryptically encoded. Rather, children are *motivated* makers of symbolic meaning right now. In their initial efforts, young children come to early literacy as creators.

In Chapter 3, Starr's lettered translation of Lori's dictation and Lori's dictation itself were not some sort of facsimile or direct mirroring of a preexisting lettered reality. Instead, both girls brought their own motivations, understandings, and artistry to the act of alphabetic creation. Indeed, Starr's painting of letters and Lori's single letter typing (including her presence and interest in the activity) manifested their idiosyncratic histories with the signs and symbols of language. Starr, Lori, and their peers were not waiting for or acquiring stable sign systems; they were constantly *in the act of making and transforming* symbolic and representational meaning. They were crafting and enacting signs out of what is made available or what might be wrenched from their surrounding worlds.

The child's transformational literate activity and its developing sophistication are manifestations of the child's citizenship in the inclusive early childhood literate community. To reiterate, this dynamic flow is composed of 1) the child's symbolic presence; 2) the narratives crafted by the child through which the surrounding world is imagined and symbolically transformed into meaningful constructs through a connectedness with others; and 3) the multiple visual, graphic, or tactile sign systems created and enacted by the child allowing for the interpretation or conveyance of narratives.

My compartmentalizing of a child's literate citizenship is useful for organization and conveyance, but is, of course, somewhat fictional. As is clear from the data vignettes collected at the Bethel Nursery School described in Chapter 3, the three constructs converge, whirl, and twist apart in a potentially infinite array of entanglements and trajectories. Still, given the convoluted ebbs, currents, swirls, vortexes, and crests, dissecting a child's literate citizenship into three aspects of a general flow provides a descriptive framework for understanding. In useful fashion, we might follow the social drive to construct symbolic sense into the narratives through which meaning is made and from there into the sign systems that allow for representation and communication.

THE CHILD'S SYMBOLIC PRESENCE

The grand debates over literacy tend to focus on story versus alphabet (or, put another way, meaning versus form). Which is inherent to the other? In contrast, I proposed earlier that the symbolic presence is the primordial stew of the young child's literate citizenship from which narrative and signs emerge. It is a child's deepest motivation to develop a connectedness with others in order to transform the surrounding world into one of symbol-based personal coherence and meaning.

Joey, a child with autism, was described in Chapter 3 as hovering at the periphery of the fantasy play area where a rocket ship made from a large box stood. Rather than seeing his actions as nonsensical, Joey's teachers and his friend Duane demonstrated local understanding in their interpretation of his actions as seeking connection, meaning, and participation through play. "We cannot understand how children find their way into printed language," noted Kress, "unless we understand the principles of their meaning-making" (1997, p. xvii).

If there exists only a singular point of agreement among influential thinkers in the psychological arena of child development, it is that young children are motivated and driven to collaboratively make symbolic meaning of their surrounding world. "Such otherwise disparate scholars as Jean Piaget, Heinz Werner, Alexander Luria, and Jerome Bruner would all concur" noted Gardner (1991, p. 58).

Piaget (1973), for instance, in describing his approach to preschool education as "constructivist" (p. 10), suggested the need to "place all educational stress on the spontaneous aspects of the child's activity" (p. 11). This reflected his deeply rooted empirical belief that the young child's self-directed action (when in a thoughtful environment) was always toward meaning-making. "For the preschool child," Piaget expressed, "to understand is to discover...and such [early educational] conditions must be complied with if individuals are to be formed who are capable of production and creativity" (p. 20). In essence, Piaget argued that preschool and kindergarten education must follow children's spontaneous, motivated drives to construct meaning within thoughtfully structured environments providing responsive guidance.

Lev Vygotsky's influence on the field of child development has only expanded throughout the West since his suppression by Stalin and early death in the 1930s in the Soviet Union. Vygotsky empirically proposed that the child's drive to construct meaning originated in his or her connectedness with the surrounding social world. "Any higher mental functions [i.e., sense-making]," stated a translation from Vygotsky's original Russian, "was external and social before it was internal. It was once a social relationship" (1981, p. 163).

This proposition formed Vygotsky's *General Genetic Law of Cultural Development*, which is "Any function in the child's psychological development appears twice or on two planes. It appears first between people as an intermental category, and then within the child as an intramental category" (1981, p. 163). Vygotsky recognized that one's biology provided a substratum for the possible path to an individual's potential to make meaning but did not determine its holistic or social nature. That fullness and directionality was dialectically influenced through relationships with the child's social web.

Social Paths Toward Meaning

Vygotsky demonstrated that a child's developing capacity to make symbolic meaning developed and flourished from his or her symbolic presence or drive to participate in culturally based social relationships. In these relationships, a child initially experiences and ultimately internalizes such sign-based higher-order operations as categorization, classification, generalization and abstraction, fantasy, counterintuition, questioning, and humor. For instance, in Chapter 3, Joey's fledgling capacity with fantasy play at the Bethel Rocket required his participation in a context that included the symbols and activity of fantasy play. All the genetic potential in the universe could not have allowed Joey to become a pretend astronaut if he had not been in a context where such fantasy play existed. Of equal necessity to the presence of play was a context organized on local understanding that supported Joey's idiosyncratic actions as evidence of his capacity to imagine alongside his peers. For many children with autism or other significant developmental disabilities, their actions serve only as evidence justifying educational and community segregation.

To use another sign-based higher-order operation as an example, Oliver Sacks (1989) pointed out that a child's capacity to attain counterintuitive truth requires participation in the patterns of effective questioning. "The origin of questioning, of an active and questioning disposition in the mind," Sacks explained, "is not something that arises spontaneously, or directly from the impact of experience; it stems, it is stimulated by communicative exchange—it requires dialogue" (p. 64). The construction of meaning on the part of children might be described from a Vygotskian vantage point as a child's transformation of the social and cultural into the internal and individualized. We are less a socialized individual creature, according to Vygotsky, than we are an individualized social creature.

Although all children are said to strive for coherence and the construction of meaning within the social web, no child's development replicates any other child's. We do not evolve or move into a stable symbolic realm that exists apart from us merely awaiting our discovery, mastery, conformity, and mimicry. Rather, we actively construct and transform our world into one of symbolic sense based on a conflux of factors—from the substratum of an individual's genetics to differentiated histories, experiences, encounters, and interactions.

The Active Role of the Child in the Construction of Meaning

Internalization of the social is truly transformative and is not a reductive process in which the personal mirrors an objective social reality. "The social does not become individual by a process of simple transmission," explained Daniels (1996), a prominent neo-Vygotskian. "Individuals construct their own sense from socially available meanings" (p. 10). In Chapter 1, Isaac found comfort in a doll representing a character from the storybook *Where the Wild Things Are*. Isaac's peer, Trevor, had requested the doll, but when told by their teacher why Isaac should hold it, Trevor appeared sympathetic. This was Isaac's first day, after all, and the doll was providing him some comfort. Trevor then pretended to chat with the doll, whereby he socially engaged Isaac. This brought a smile and a response from Isaac, which was his first real interaction with a friend in the new setting. Trevor appeared to be making empathic sense from Isaac's initial uncertainty, and Isaac, through Trevor's unique, directed, and specific efforts, gained a foothold of stability in the unfamiliar context.

The instruments that allow for cultural individualization (what Vygotsky termed the *tools of mediation*) are signs and sign systems. The primary sign system engaged by children in their construction of meaning is language. Vygotsky emphasized spoken language, much to the detriment of children whose spoken language is difficult to decipher. He suggested that children and adults engage sign systems that emphasize speech to enter relationships, direct one another's social activity, and, eventually, direct (or mediate) their own social activity. The self-talk of early childhood becomes silent, internal language as sophistication develops. Other mediating sign systems develop as the child both encounters them and encounters the cultural need to make use of them.

THE CHILD'S CONSTRUCTION OF NARRATIVE

The symbolic presence bubbles, steams, and erupts into the world of signs and symbols through narrative. Narrative refers to (by degree) the structured crafting and shaping of experience, autobiography, biography, ideas, thoughts, concerns, interests, desires, emotions, visions, fantasies, and stories. "Children very quickly come to understand that content has a shape," noted Kress (1997), "a socially given pattern that varies by type" (p. 119). In Chapter 1, I described the Corner Nook's daily ritual of circle time. Children entered into this ritual through the construction of various narrative configurations symbolically reflecting interests. Some children bounded over excitedly and became engaged in the teacher's agenda. Two girls walked hand-in-hand, excluding a third girl and maintaining this ostracizing pose throughout the period. Some of the students groaned in resistance to the teacher imposition of formal structure that ended the preceding playtime.

Even when children are said to be *receiving* or *consuming*, rather than constructing, a narrative (e.g., listening to the book *Where the Wild Things Are*), they are in fact in the act of creating, crafting, and shaping a narrative. That is, they are linking the other person's (e.g., author Maurice Sendak's) narrative to their own stories. Upon entering the character Max's world of boats and monsters, children drag their own worlds along. Gallas described this process as

> Projecting ourselves into another space, another time, another framework. To read a text with understanding and insight, we must move inside the text, pulling our life along with us and incorporating the text and our lives into a new understanding of the world. (2003, p. 20)

Narratives may be told, made sense of, understood, retold, and altered such that a symbolic connectedness or a literate community is crafted through the shared meaning children construct. McEwan and Egan contend that at the heart of all literacy is visually accessible narrative:

> Narrative is basically extended language configured in such a way that its earlier embodiment in life [e.g., a thought, an emotion] becomes *revealed* [i.e., is made visual, graphic, or tactual]....What distinguishes narrative is that it takes shape in however *attenuated a form*, as a rhythm that ultimately springs from patterns implicit in human life and action. (1995, p. vii, emphasis added)

No general consensus exists in the literature on child development as to what precisely constitutes a narrative (Riessman, 2000). McEwan, and Egan (1995) have suggested that a narrative includes a subject (e.g., some form of "I") from whose perspective something is expressed in a structure that is both understandable to an audience and carries with it a pattern containing affective force. A particular narrative might be fairly enduring, as the story within a child's completed drawing that is then sent home and reexpressed (albeit never exactly the same) for the parent, or highly attenuated, as the fantasy play occurring in a box designated to be a rocket. Early sign-based movement toward narrative begins with the child's naming of the world and quickly moves into categorization and classification. Classification requires the recognition that something is like something else or can be logically represented by some other object. It is the young child's first dramatic foray into metaphor—a fundamental aspect of written language and all other sign systems in which symbols stand for something else.

For young children, the developing capacity to classify and categorize spills into their use of signs to describe recurrent events is commonly referred to among developmental psychologists as the use of *scripts* (Heath, 1983, p. 5). Children are quick studies of routines. They are able to realize key components that make up, for instance, a birthday party or a bedtime ritual. Scripts serve as the origins of narrative and storytelling, which allow children to conceptualize and report on what has occurred in daily life. Scripts also serve as a generic blueprint against which new encounters and opportunities are judged, understood, and, in symbolic and sign-based fashion, internalized.

Because the making of meaning through narratives is considered fundamental and built on naming, categorizing, and scripting, these actions are commonly cast as *universals*, applicable to all children. The imagery associated with universals unfortunately binds such operations to one of two forms of determinism. That is, children's narrative capacities are said to unfold according to either biological dictates or rigid, culturally contrived molds. Again, the debate here is moot. In flawed fashion, the contesting frameworks act to pacify the child's agency. I am suggesting a contrasting sense of the child's drive to make meaning as motivated, self-determined, purposeful, intelligent, and uniquely transformative.

Even when the narratives of a particular child appear to be very similar to that of other children, each child brings his or her personal experiences and multiple histories to bear. In Chapter 1, for instance, when Isaac joined his peers at circle time to listen to the teacher read *Where the Wild Things Are*, the narratives that flowed from the children's efforts to make sense of the character Max being sent to his room appeared somewhat alike, but they actually reflected deeply individualized scripts concerning getting into trouble, naughtiness, and punishment. No child's script mirrored any other child's; nor did the scripts mirror a generic cultural or genetic script. They reflected each participating child's own life injected into the storybook narrative.

As efforts to make sense of the world develop in sophistication, the young child's creation of scripts explodes in a myriad of directions, including the realms of dramatic and pretend or fantasy play. "The narrative begins early," Paley (2004) noted, "even before the spoken word, the pictures in the young child's mind assume a storylike quality. How else could the dramatic play emerge so fully formed?" (p. 14). Paley referred to fantasy play as the "glue that binds together all [young children's] other pursuits, including the early teaching of reading and writing skills" (p. 8).

Imagination and Narrative

Imagination is the point where a child's experiences and histories converge on the present activity and explode into countless narrative possibilities that in turn alter the symbolic presence and future actions and narratives. Vygotsky (1930/2003) stated, "Imagination, as the basis of all creative activity, is an important component of absolutely all aspects of cultural life, enabling artistic, scientific, and technical creation alike" (p. 10). He continued by saying

> In this sense, absolutely everything around us that was created by the hand of man, the entire world of human culture, as distinct from the world of nature, all this is the product of human imagination and of creation based on this imagination. (1930/2003, p. 10)

In a separate essay, directly relevant to the young child's symbolic presence and narrative construction, Vygotsky (1987) proposed that intellect and imagination formed a unitary whole "inherent in a child's very first generalization" (p. 78). Thus, when a child names the world, organizes those names into categories, develops scripts, and extends scripts in either a synthesis or a myriad of directions, he or she is expressing the capacity to construct alternative futures. "We use imagination in our ordinary perception of the world," noted Warnock (1976). "This perception cannot be separated from interpretation. Interpretation can be common to everyone, and in this sense ordinary, or it can be inventive, personal, and revolutionary" (p. 10). He continued

> So imagination is necessary to enable us to recognize things in the world as familiar, to take for granted features of the world which we need to take for granted and rely on if we are to go about our ordinary business; but it is also necessary if we are to see the world as significant of something unfamiliar, if we are to treat the objects of perception as symbolizing or suggesting things other than themselves. (1976, p. 10)

Certainly some children's narratives will follow more rigidly (although will not mirror) encountered scripts (i.e., be ordinary), whereas other children will at times be more divergent in approach (revolutionary). Imagination, however, cannot be separated from the child's motivation and ultimate effort to construct meaning. "Imagination is not an empirical and superadded power of consciousness," argued Sartre (1961), "it is the whole of consciousness" (p. 270).

THE CHILD'S CONSTRUCTION OF VISUAL, ORTHOGRAPHIC, AND TACTILE SIGN SYSTEMS

In Chapter 1, I noted a group of boys generating narratives as they built roads out of wooden blocks over which they moved toy cars. I also described Isaac holding a doll representing the character, Max, from *Where the Wild Things Are* as he listened to and observed the storybook being read and discussed. Ultimately, he created a dance to go along with the story. In Chapter 3, I described Jared, Duane, and Joey playing in a box made to represent a rocket ship. Due to the efforts of Lori and Starr, the name *Bethel Raket* was painted along the side. In addition, I emphasized Joey and his teacher, Ms. Perry, writing a note to Joey's mother at the end of the day. There was also a description of a drawing made by 4-year-old Andrew in which he depicted a birthday party. These nine forms of representation and communication—the maze of block roads, toy cars, Max doll, storybook, dance, box rocket ship, painted name, note home, and drawing—are visual, orthographic, or tactile signs that capture, fix, and convey or allow for the interpretation of narratives.

Within semiotics, or the study of sign systems, the term *sign* has a rather specific definition—the combination of a particular symbol's meaning and form. The sign is neither meaning nor form; it is always the combination. Signs do not exist apart from human action. Human beings individually or collectively enact signs to craft narratives through which meaning is constructed. Thus, signs are inherently unstable in that their meaning is never detached or objective in the traditional sense of the term; they are always in transformation in the motivations, hands, and imaginations of those constructing the given narrative.

The Nine Signs

The wooden blocks used by the boys in the Corner Nook to construct a complex roadway certainly have an objective presence, as do the toy cars. Yet, only in the hands and imaginations of the children do the blocks, arranged end-to-end, take on the form and meaning of *road* as designated in the specific narrative construction I was observing. Furthermore, those same blocks used on a subsequent day, even for a very similar play scenario, will have a new meaning, slight as it might be, given an altered narrative. The sign is contingent on the actions and imaginations of the children involved. As mentioned in Chapter 1, the blocks-as-road design has profound metaphoric qualities. The blocks obviously are not a complete road, but they act as a representation of a road. Arranged in a particular way, they have enough road-like qualities. This symbolic, metaphoric representation is a central aspect of developing sophistication with language and all literacy.

The Max doll Isaac clung to was a widely available, commercial product. Clearly its designer and producer had a three-dimensional form in mind that was as close in appearance to Maurice Sendak's two-dimensional drawings as possible. As such, it can be argued that this was a sign with a given or objective form and meaning. Certainly the original crafters of the sign influenced subsequent (including Isaac's) usage, but they did not dictate nor even direct it. Isaac, for instance, individually transformed and personally shaped the sign of the Max doll based on the context of the classroom and his own history and experiences. The doll became a source of negotiation with his teacher who traded with Isaac so that she might have the book. Thus, the doll was an initial indicator of assertiveness on the part of Isaac. It also was a source of comfort in the unfamiliar territory, and, ultimately, it provided the focus for Isaac's first interaction with a peer, Trevor, who in essence spoke to Isaac through the doll.

The storybook *Where the Wild Things Are* was a sign made from multiple signs. The book had its own cumulative form and meaning composed of printed words, phrases, and pictures, all of which are themselves signs composed of form and meaning. The words, phrases, and pictures had been created by an author, Maurice Sendak, who clearly held a particular intent with his textual effort. Similar to the Max doll, this intent might be misconstrued as forming a sort of objective structure to dictate how the audience will interpret, understand, and react to the story. However, the act of reading or listening to and looking at a storybook is not merely an act of decoding or interpretation, but, rather, an act of narrative and sign creation, construction, and transformation. Children do not merely move into some preset mold; they actively work to construct meaning by linking the original author's efforts to their own context, histories, and experiences. In effect, from the signs provided (meaning and form) they create new signs.

In their effort to make sense of the world, in this case a preexisting story, young children craft signs from the crafted signs of others. Heath (1986) describes this interactional view of the writer and reader as the "cocreation" of an "interdependent text" (p. 156). Cocreation is always a subjective process. Multiple children may experience a preexisting story in very similar fashion (hence they may construct very similar signs and narratives), but no two children ever experience a story exactly alike (as such, even very similar constructed signs and narratives are not exactly alike).

At one point in *Where the Wild Things Are*, the character Max, as king of the wild things, declares to the monsters that the rumpus should begin. His proclamation initiates a series of three beautiful illustrations, each covering two complete pages, depicting Max and the Wild Things in various *Lord-of-the-Flies*-like stages of dance, marching, and general hooliganism. As an ethnographer, I watched Isaac focus with intensity on his teacher as she read and turned the pages. Isaac sat with legs crossed, hands clenched around the Max doll held tightly in his lap, and body leaning in toward the book. With each new page he leaned a bit farther until his neighbor, Trevor, actually squirmed to readjust his position to see the pictures. When the page opened to the rumpus, Isaac pushed himself to his feet, thrust his arm into the air, spread his feet, spun awkwardly, attempted a jump, stumbled, bumped against a surprised peer, regained his footing, thrust back his head, and continued on with his dance.

Isaac's teacher, Ms. Robbins, brought the book down slightly. Her eyes widened. An associate teacher sitting amid the children put her hand over her mouth to hide a smile. All of the students gazed with a degree of wonder toward their new addition who appeared lost in his art, oblivious to the momentary pause. Ms. Robbins, a quintessential model of local understanding, immediately read the situation and called out, "Isaac has the rumpusing moves! Who else can 'rumpus?'" With the book held open over her head, she along with other adults and children, joined Isaac in his spinning, marching, and shaking. I sat toward the back of the room and jotted down the note, "Did not know you can dance to books at all."

Isaac's dance was his wonderful construction of a sign, its form and meaning inextricably intertwined. As described in Chapter 2, young children's expressions reside on a continuum running from communicative to representational. Speech (or spoken signs) is the primary mode of young children's communication, whereas visual, orthographic, or tactile signs are, initially, the primary mode of representation.

Emphasizing communication suggests the young child's chief concern is with choosing signs that are most apt to be understood by a particular audience. Emphasizing representation suggests the young child crafts the most apt signs (given materials available) to reflect an idea or emotion with less regard for an audience. Communication is most focused on the audience, and representation is most focused on the maker. By no means is either exclusionary of the other.

As children age, schools tend to emphasize communication over representation, and sanctioned sign systems narrow and are shifted into this effort. In the Corner Nook classroom, however, where multiple sign systems and motivations were valued, Isaac's dance could be seen as primarily representation. It also demonstrated that Isaac was able to follow the story, interpret written and/or read and illustrated events, symbolically participate in the story through the construction of signs, and draw his peers into his own unique representation.

Similar to the storybook and Isaac's dance, the Bethel Nursery School rocket ship, constructed from a refrigerator box and sundry parts, was a complex sign composed of a multitude of subsidiary signs that were glued, taped, or cut into the interior space. These included labels, drawings, and pictures clipped from magazines representing gears, switches, and computers; portholes covered by blue transparent paper; and various gadgets and wires the students and adults associated with space flight. Combined with the spoken language, actions, and gestures composing the fantasy narratives inspired by space flight, the rocket area of the classroom clearly demonstrated children's use of multiple sign systems within a single narrative. Young children never rely on a single sign system, but always synthesize systems making use of what is available to most aptly, wholly, and satisfactorily construct the emergent narrative.

The meaning of the rocket at Bethel changed in emphasis depending on the particular narrative crafters making use of the form. For instance, an arguably gendered transition took place when Emily and Robyn took over the interior of the box by bringing in several dolls representing a family in space. The box retained its metaphoric quality of being rocketlike and serving as a symbol of space travel, but as a sign it was inherently unstable in that individual children were constantly negotiating and renegotiating distinct and unique meanings based on contesting and competing motivations, histories, and experiences.

Friends Starr and Lori, under the guidance of a teacher's aide, had christened in paint the Bethel rocket. Their lettered creation capturing the narrative of naming the rocket was a sign composed of smaller signs (i.e., the individual letters chosen by Lori and depicted with lavish flair by Starr) and was constitutive of the larger sign of the complete Bethel rocket.

The note Joey co-constructed with his teacher at the end of the school day was designed to provide the child with an opportunity to reflect on his day, summarize particular aspects into a narrative, and translate those aspects into an orthographic-based sign interpretable by others. His teacher provided him with prewritten options, some of which also included somewhat abstract symbols. Joey's participation suggested he understood the nature of the narrative he was crafting, and his gestures suggested a developing skill with recognizing printed words.

Andrew's drawn depiction of his brother's birthday party was again a sign composed of arranged (sub)signs. When he sat down at the table containing markers and paper, the raw materials of his efforts, it appeared he had the birthday narrative in mind. He immediately grabbed a blue marker and said out loud, "His cake is always blue. Mommy makes the cake blue," and he drew a slightly rounded square shape with several long lines coming out of the top (explaining later that they were candles). He then switched markers and began to draw characters representing people. The depictions were stereotypical early childhood characters with heads resting on long legs without torsos.

Despite this seemingly universal preschool approach to figure drawing, there was nothing universal about the individual intent and motivation of Andrew. He had his own unique story to tell and, although his signs might have resembled the signs of another child, they were demonstrably his own, born of his own symbolic presence and specific narrative. He crafted what he described as the figure of his mother and then drew over that figure, a head shorter and enveloped in the mother's body, another figure. "This is me," he later explained. The figure he made of his brother was actually leaning in toward the hovering blue cake. Andrew drew a circle within the circle head to represent an open mouth. He announced, "He's eating the cake."

The circles, similar to other signs, served as metaphors. Humans are not only heads, but the heads in Andrew's drawing were the most prominent feature along with lines for legs. Heads largely represented humans. Furthermore, human heads are not shaped exactly like circles, but Andrew had learned that circles have enough "head quality" to be used as a symbolic representation. Others would understand his efforts. Again, mouths are not circles, but circles drawn within circles that represent heads may be mouths. Circles are mouth-like enough, and, therefore, can symbolize the idea of mouth.

Several minutes into the artistic endeavor Andrew began adding drawn, recognizable letters alongside squiggles that were also intended as letters. He was adding captions to explain his drawing and, therefore, delving into a new sign system. Later, his teacher would extend this by writing across the bottom of the picture, "Andrew's brother's birthday party." I observed Andrew staring at the sentence for several seconds, perhaps internalizing its location on the page as a powerful communicator of his representational intent.

The Trajectory of Early Literate Citizenship

From the infinite potential of the inclusive terrain, children actively construct, transform, and create a sign-based literate community out of visual, orthographic, or tactile symbols and systems. Signs express narratives. A sign is a combination of meaning and form. Meaning is the essence of what a sign signifies. Form is the signifier—the visual, tactile, or auditory *shape* used to do the signifying.

The child's traverse from playing in a box rocket to writing out *Bethel Raket* is commonly captured in a metaphoric sense as the very story of literacy itself. Gallas (2003) described this symbolic movement as "from playing to drawing to writing" (p. 42). Conventional theories suggest the path is one that takes a child from highly representational and unstable sign systems to an ever more singular, abstract, arbitrary, stable, mechanistic, and conventional system. At the moment of its construction, the large box held the critical features required of the Bethel children for it to symbolize and function as a rocket. The material form of the box, with some additions and modifications, became an apt medium for the expression of the meaning *rocket*. We can describe this as highly representational in that the meaning of the sign is revealed in its form. Meaning is intrinsic to form, and form is intrinsic to meaning.

In early childhood, the meaning and form of signs are commonly indistinguishable. This makes them representational but also clearly unstable and nonmechanistic in that the signs are context bound or, put another way, highly influenced by the specific social network in which the sign is crafted. Another group of children crafting a rocket in a setting apart from Bethel would create a different sign with different narratives attached even when presented with the same materials. The ultimate product might be similar but would not be a clone or copy.

In contrast, the written word r-o-c-k-e-t is composed of particular letters arranged in a conventional and rule-laden sequence and structure that does not reveal its meaning without an adult pointing it out to children. The presumption pervades that in written language, unlike in other early childhood sign systems, form and meaning have no intrinsic connection. Form then is said to be arbitrary, plucked from the great ether just as Adam is described in the book of Genesis randomly ascribing names for the birds, fish, and animals. Furthermore, the word *rocket* in one setting is commonly considered to be *rocket* in all settings that share in the English language. As such, spelling out or deciphering rocket is said to be an abstraction or, in other words, is context-free. The sign is commonly thought to transcend individual or collective imagination and, therefore, might be considered stable or mechanical.

Together, these presumed but flawed foundational factors of written language—bound to convention, rule-laden, arbitrary, abstract, mechanistic, stable—result in formal early literacy programs that ignore the inherent instability (i.e., context or person-bound nature) of all signs as well as young children's motivations, experiences, histories, and, amazingly, their actual efforts with multiple sign systems including, from very young ages, written language. Rather, as formal literacy programs pervade the lives of ever-younger children, literacy (and language in general) is treated as a distinct and rigid structure apart and autonomous from children toward which they must intellectually conform through teacher-directed drill. This occurs initially around the form of written language and later around its meaning.

Metaphorically and realistically, children do expand in their sign-based capacity from *playing rocket* to express a narrative to *writing r-o-c-k-e-t* to accomplish the same. In loose fashion this does seem to follow a patterned route, albeit one that is always highly individualized and never linear, from the sign systems of play to drawing to written language. This would suggest, however, that written language is not some contrived code culturally manufactured apart from the earlier symbol expression of young children but is instead an intertwined, recursive extension and inversion of those systems.

Despite the origin, we know that young children do not approach sign systems as if they were capriciously arbitrary, hopelessly abstract, and convolutedly convention bound. Neither are children prone to wait while natural processes emerge from within. Rather, given whatever materials are available, children actively and with strident purpose intertwine meaning and form in a transformative manner that best expresses by communication or representation the particular narrative of the moment. When a large box appears in the inclusive preschool classroom, children flock to it with stories of space flight, voyages on the ocean, forts to defend, and babies to care for at home. The box transformed into a sign contains the critical features required to inspire and further various children's narratives.

Shifting from the expression of narratives in three dimensions to two dimensions begins extremely early in children's lives. From birth they are immersed in two-dimensional narratives made up of various combinations containing photos, text, drawings, storybooks, retail and restaurant signs, billboards, magazines, and so forth. If the signs are unnecessary to the child's motivated efforts with the construction of meaning, then they are ignored or relegated to background noise. Often, however, two-dimensional signs are central to a child's ability to make sense. For instance, a child's efforts to be like mommy (i.e., entering the adult world) might at times involve acting out the part of reading a magazine or newspaper. So the child holds and reads his or her own version of a paper and for a moment becomes mommy. Provided opportunity and resources, research has consistently shown that children as young as 2 years make purposeful, determined marks on paper (or other less appropriate materials!) that contain narrative significance and meaning.

As with two-dimensional signs in general, children encounter written language from birth. Part of the drive to make sense of the world is making sense of printed language, and children do so, as in all areas, in a motivated, sense-filled manner. Printed language is not some mysterious code that floats in mirage-like fashion on the child's horizon; it is immediate and attached to the child. A 4-year-old in an inclusive preschool classroom handed me a sheet with several squiggly lines plus some seemingly recognizable letters drawn in a row.

"Read this," she said.

I said, "Why don't you read it to me?"

She said, "No, you read it." I stumbled over the letters to form some phonetic representation. She said, "No, try it this way," pointing from left to right across the sequence of letters.

I said, "That's how I did read it," and I repeated my previous effort.

"Well, try it this way," she said, this time pointing from right to left. I attempted a backward pronunciation. With a palpable degree of annoyance, she took the sheet and pointed to the left side of the row. "It says," she said, "I love Lena" [a best friend in the class]. In addition to her written message, she was also saying, "I am in charge of this sign system. I can transform two-dimensional line, shape, and space to tell my story."

Children's early drawings are often complex stories. They are, in essence, *writing* pictures. Embedded within children's drawings are the lines and squiggles that reflect first forays into constructing printed words as part of the process of constructing meaning. These early efforts in printed language are, in essence, *drawing* words. Children write pictures and draw words (see Kress, 1997). Both are central to literacy. As with other sign systems, children are attempting to capture critical features of the narrative in question through the meaning and form chosen. The signs of printed language are no different in relation to the child's motivation and effort than the three-dimensional signs of play. Kress noted,

> The learning of writing proceeds in exactly the same fashion as the development of other sign systems: employing the strategy of using the best, most apt available form of expression of a particular meaning. Children use such representational means as they have available for making that meaning. The child's written signs are the effect of their meaning making actions, arising out of interest, using what they have available as representational means. (1997, p. 17)

Whether the child expresses great care or frenetic impulsiveness in the creation and interpretation of written signs, he or she is never acting in an arbitrary or mechanistic manner but is always symbolically communicating or representing interest, perception, thought, and affective motivation. The child's symbolic presence is percolating through narrative into the visual, orthographic, or tactile realm of signs.

In the developing capacity to represent and interpret narrative within two-dimensional written language, children commonly make the shift from acting out or drawing ideas directly (e.g., crayon figures representing people at a birthday party) to *drawing words* to *drawing sounds*. By *drawing sounds*, I mean that the child must use the crayon to form the shape of letters that, clustered together, represent the sound of the particular idea or object being represented or communicated. (Detailed studies described in Chapter 5 suggest that for some children this shift may actually deemphasize sound and continue to emphasize meaning, but, nonetheless, at some level the child does begin to recognize relationships between the sign system of speech and orthographic sign systems.)

The English alphabet originated, as did all alphabetic systems, in pictographic or hieroglyphic script; that is, abstracted and reduced images evolved and came to stand for sounds. Within pictographic systems, written characters are directly representative of ideas; only as a second step are ideas translated into sound. In alphabetic script, however, the first translation is commonly conceived as being from *written word* into *spoken word* (sound), and not until the second step do we arrive at the idea.

No evidence exists to suggest that either translative sequence—pictographic or alphabetic—is inherently more difficult to learn. However, children appear to be natural, or unschooled, pictographers; therefore, convention ascribes a certain rudimentary, even native, quality to their pictorial representations while pointing out that their capacity to alphabetically scribe requires formal schooling. According to the conventional logic, alphabetic writing must be unnatural and therefore more complex.

This logic, however, may not be true. First, when very young children are provided the opportunity, they may begin writing long before adults impose formal literacy programs. However, children's representational figure drawings and certainly their play might be more recognizable to an audience of adults who focus on their art or acting as intentional, meaningful, and clearly natural and dismiss other markings on the canvas as extraneous, unintentional, or irrational. Young children whose spoken language is just emerging are able to make marks (signs) on paper that qualitatively vary when an adult makes the request to draw a story versus draw numbers to count (Lancaster, 2003). This is one of many indicators that early marks might actually be purposeful signs with narrative significance. Just as a child's pictures grow in representational sophistication and communicative complexity, so, too, do the marks that we might associate with alphabetic print. At some point, the adult audience begins to recognize these efforts as alphabetic, but perhaps the child begins this movement long before parents or teachers are prepared to acknowledge it.

Second, formal school curricula that begin in kindergarten or even earlier sanction and regulate a very rigid version of alphabetic script while dismissing or, at best, diminishing children's efforts with other graphic, visual, or tactile systems. Of course, these other sign systems can be of equal sophistication and importance alongside written language. Yet, because they are not treated as such in the formalities of the educational system, we are culturally instilled with a sense that they are less valuable, worthwhile, meaningful, and, ultimately, less complex and useful. Thus, rigid versions of alphabetic signs become the *real stuff* of schooling, and for many children other sign systems are grouped as nonintellectual and nonessential and fade into the background.

Nevertheless, well before young children enter school, they begin to transform written language into their own expressive system. In so doing, they come to understand a number of critical factors about the written word that are conceptually distinct, but no more complex, from pictographic processes. Children see adults spending time staring at, engaging in, commenting on, or creating lines of text, either through writing or on the computer. When children look at picture books with adults, the picture may cover a large territory, but usually the adult spends an inordinate amount of time on the relatively isolated text. A child may ask about a picture in a newspaper and then notice the adult shifting to the text to provide a full explanation.

The text clearly steers the story just as the visual images steer the story. However, in a child's mind, the two might not automatically converge, and it would appear to the child that the adult prioritizes the textual interpretation of the narrative over the visual one. A child may ask, "What is that a picture of?" to which the adult responds, "It looks like a wolf. Let's read to find out." The child quickly comes to recognize that those particular marks or characters must be extremely important and that when put together they represent a narrative text that contains tremendous authority.

The textual meaning or story that is caught and fixed within and through alphabetic signs is the central facet of the young child's earliest engagement with printed language. "What does this say?" they ask of written words encountered or marks they themselves have strung together. In essence, they are asking for the embedded story or textual meaning. Although the syntax or form of a printed sentence is clearly important, young children recognize and are motivated by the story or function of the sentence. Any approach to early literacy must start here where children themselves begin the effort—with adults and children together opening up the meaning or narrative of the clustered alphabetic signs. Of course, individual children are going to be drawn to different stories and different narratives. What catches the fascination of one child will differ for another. Each is developing a unique literate profile.

Unfortunately, conventional early literacy programs and assessments ignore children's motivations to make meaning, as well as the individual nature of those motivations. Instead, formal literacy efforts frame written language as if it were foremost a convoluted web of nearly impenetrable syntactical coding rules and patterns that all children must memorize in exact, mechanistic fashion prior to the development of a story. Once a child demonstrates enough rudimentary skills associated with print or reaches a certain age, sounds, letters, letter-combinations, and written sentences are stripped of their meaning and presented as conventional, mechanized patterns. Children's motivation to make sense and construct meaning—their literate actions to date—are disregarded as inconsequential. In essence, like a boot camp for tots, they are stripped of their literacy, taught that they are illiterate (or, more aptly, preliterate), and slowly over years built back up in the literate mold of schooling. Many will fail in this endeavor.

In contrast, lead teacher Ms. Robbins at the Shoshone School told me in a research interview,

> I see all my kids as readers. My hardest job is to get them to see themselves as readers. Somehow by [age] 4 they've learned they're not [readers] and it's harder than hell to convince them otherwise. But it's amazing when you do!

Teachers who approach children's earliest literacy as textually (i.e., meaning) motivated are able to follow children's drive and interest in learning to control, order, and organize written language signs in ever more conventional (or understandable) patterns to express a narrative. In essence they move from text to letter, from large unit to small, and from drawing whole phrases and words to drawing sounds (Kress, 1997). This is in opposition to convention, which starts with sound, moves to letter, and only later arrives at words, phrases, and, ultimately, meaning. Teachers show and children participate in developing the concept that meaning might be drawn in patterned letters providing a particular orthographic shape. We see children experiment with these shapes by attaching them together in new arrangements. In these experiments, sometimes children will initiate leaving behind the conceptual sense of the sign system and focus instead on its spatial, visual, and phonemic qualities. The line of print momentarily stops *meaning*, and its structure or form takes center stage.

In these early experiments, the child may continue to shift back and forth between meaning and form. The making of symbols and markings and eventually invented spelling are a child's earnest and directed efforts to combine lettered form and meaning to express a narrative. The earliest efforts here often appear *random* in that adults struggle to decipher the created marks and shapes, but the child is never acting in random fashion. There is always intention and meaning, whether it is silly or serious or something in between. As the child increases in conventional competence with the alphabet, invented spelling grows in sophistication. For instance, at a classroom writing table, two 4-year-old girls sat side by side, each working diligently on a story about pizza. One drew a circle containing a sort of triangle and the semblance of a *P* hovering nearby. The other took great care in writing out *P-Z-Z-Z-A*.

Whereas the former girl was engaging primarily in pictography, the latter child recognized that groups of letters clustered and aligned from left to right could represent an idea and had a sense of which shapes went with which sound. She used her logic then to sequence and present the letters. In addition, she probably had visually noticed from previous experience, including a group activity that had just occurred, that the word pizza had more than one *z*. For a child interested in letters, a double *z* might be fairly dramatic and noticeable. She then translated that drama into three *z*s. This girl appeared not to be sounding out the word, but rather drawing it from having internalized its shape as if it was a pictographic effort. She was drawing the orthographic shape of the written word *pizza* to represent the idea of pizza.

For the two girls, we could describe the term and idea of pizza as a momentary problem to solve. "How will we best depict *pizza* on this paper?" the girls might ponder. The girls each had a unique literate profile and arrived in distinct fashion at a plausible solution. In a preceding activity, both girls had just seen the word *pizza* written correctly and sounded out by a teacher. Neither, however, copied the adult's version. Each transformed the word into her own sign based on experience, sensibility, skill with shape, and so forth.

I observed teachers taking advantage of the children's fascination with meaning and form by bringing out both at the same time. Following a field trip that inspired these two students, their teacher wrote on a paper strip several feet long, "We visited the pizza restaurant and ate breadsticks and pizza!" Her 4-year-old students watched with rapt attention. She then cut the strip into its separate words and had the children take turns rearranging the story into *silly sentences*.

"What does this say?" a boy yelled.

The teacher read, "Visited breadsticks we pizza pizza and and restaurant the ate!" The children laughed.

The teacher called out, "Which words say *pizza*?" A girl sprang forward and pointed correctly. "How did you know?"

"'Cause they're the same," the girl replied.

Another girl answered, "They start with *P.*"

A boy joined in, "Pizza is for *P.*"

Another child said, "They's got the 'zees' in them."

Through rich experience, young children develop the sense that there exists a relationship between the spoken and written forms of language. They begin to understand that particular, repeatable shapes constitute letters that can be grouped into words. Children without significant disabilities formulate emergent ideas about the relationship between letters and sounds, and they begin to associate correct shapes with their matched sounds. (The importance of this and its relationship to young children with significant developmental disabilities is discussed in Chapter 5.)

Children develop a spatial sense that text occurs in lines or organized blocks. Furthermore, the organized blocks of text vary from spoken language. In the semiotics of speech, meaning is sequenced in time with clauses following clauses. Sequence, repetition, restatement, and reformulation are all central aspects of speech. In writing, meaning is organized visually in space (e.g., across a page), and clauses may be embedded within other clauses, with some being main clauses and others subordinate.

Written language may be more complex than spoken language. Children quickly learn that written stories inherently sound different than do spoken stories. Although this is an issue of structure, it also is one of sound. When a child pretends to be a teacher, the inflection and tonal qualities of his or her voice change, sometimes becoming more automatonic or, conversely, more emotive when *reading* a picture book to whatever audience of dolls, stuffed animals, or peers surround him or her.

As I have previously pointed out, both a child's use of signs to convey narratives *and* his or her interpretation of signs that give shape to the narratives created by others are acts of transformation on the part of the child. No narrative ever wholly replicates another. As such, no sequenced signs ever replicate another set, and, given children's unique histories, no individual sign within the sequence will ever have the precise meaning of another child's sign, even when they are seemingly the same. Think of how the idea and meaning of *dog* varies from child to child. As such, signs, even those that follow convention, are never wholly stable or mechanistic; instead, they are always context bound.

Certainly there may be great similarities across narratives, but there is always a degree of transformation in the act of narrative formation. For instance, from Chapter 3, when Ms. Lee, a teacher's aide at Bethel Nursery School, asked Starr and Lori to name the rocket ship, Starr blurted out, "Bethel Rocket!" The name may not appear original, and other children might have made the same choice, but the underlying logic of how Starr arrived at that name was hers alone. What personal experiences led Starr to suggest that vessels be named after the community from which they come? Starr's path to naming the rocket was unique to her own experience. Even though children may end up at a point similar to other children, it is always by way of an individualized route.

Neither was Lori's typing of the name to guide Starr's painting of the letters an act of mimicry. It was transformative and unique to Lori's history. First, she had noticed the pattern associated with the word Bethel. Although every child in the classroom had been given the same opportunity to notice this pattern, few others had. Lori gravitated toward understanding sequenced letters in ways considered unusual for a 4-year-old. Second, when she articulated the term *Bethel* on her Dynavox, she had her own set of meanings associated with it based on her very individualized experience in the classroom. In this sense, she was not copying the sign *Bethel* but was creating it in new form to fit her current and, perhaps, momentary needs. As such, we might conclude that the sign *Bethel* and the individual, subsidiary signs from which it was constructed are not stable or abstract and context free, but are always the result of individual transformation. On the surface, one child's use of the sign *Bethel* may appear extremely similar to another child's, but they always follow individual paths.

The interpretation of the signs of another's text (e.g., reading, being read to, looking at pictures) is also the construction of signs. Previously, I pointed out how the children's reactions (i.e., their construction of new signs) varied in response to the picture book *Where the Wild Things Are*. Children are not simply decoding some objective meaning when confronting an existing text, but are always in the process of translating and connecting the text to their own experiences as a way of making sense of the narrative and the world. In the example of the two girls participating in the group activity following a visit to a pizza restaurant, each took the original narrative and crafted new and very original signs with their own unique narratives.

Crafting new signs, whether through the direct construction of text or through the interpretation of another's text, provides children with a developing sophistication of written language. They are learning that the signs they create are not haphazard or random but hold a particular logic and that the motivated link between meaning and form is maintained as they move into alphabetic text. Meaning remains the integral element, and form is the means of expression. Marks that are closely connected contain meaning, and there is a formal organization (i.e., linkages and lines of text) that allows for the organization of meaning. Children experience written language as having particular *spatial qualities, layout,* and *directionality*. They also encounter it as *linear*, as elements in *sequence*, as sequenced elements that are *connected*, as elements made up of *simple shapes*, and as elements that are *repeatable*. There appears to be no rooted or native hierarchy here. Children in inclusive, literate communities are exposed to these complexities, actively engage in them, and begin to construct meaning from them in different patterns, at different rates, and according to individualized literate profiles. Although literacy may appear similar across children, no two children ever follow the same path or pattern.

Beginning with Words of Intense Meaning

Children's earliest efforts at making sense of the complexities of print tend to be around signs of particular significance and meaning. Children learn that meaning and form are maintained in alphabetic signs. Often the child's printed name is one word that is central to the child's identity and is made visually available in the early childhood environment with commentary from surrounding adults.

Early in the school year, just prior to his fourth birthday, I observed Sam, a typically developing child, sign his name. He made a line with several curves considered by his teachers to represent an *S*. He told an adult, "This is Sam. This is me! I drew my name." Sam had come at that moment to symbolically embody a sense of self in the beginning letter of his name. In addition, he had spent an extraordinary amount of time developing the curves of the *S*. If I had not been observing, I would have assumed he had made the line quickly and fairly randomly. However, I had been witness to the intellectual intensity that he poured into the effort. Clearly the shape was of central concern, even though it bore only minimal similarity to what I consider a normal *S*.

Some of Sam's peers were also demonstrating interest in letter formation to express narratives. Some focused their creative efforts on the linear quality of lines of text; others grouped markings together in a way that looked like single words but were at times read as sentences. Still others seemed to be, similar to Sam, interested in the intricacies of certain letter shapes. No two children were exactly alike. Each was developing a unique literate profile.

It might be inferred that Sam's drawn *S* has no inherent representational qualities of Sam and is thus an arbitrary symbol randomly attached to the beginning phoneme of his name. Such a frame of mind might lead to the conclusion that drill and rote memorization are rational approaches to literacy and that Sam will *get better* at literacy as he grows. In contrast, the vital point is that Sam did not approach his written name as arbitrary, but rather he had come to purposefully, emotionally, and intellectually embody the symbols in an extraordinarily motivated manner. This process clearly began long before any formal literacy program was imposed. The *S* was the whole of Sam. At this point he was not drawing sound, but, instead, he was drawing meaning using certain letters to represent not particular phonemes but the essence of his representation.

To better understand Sam's literate *S*, recall that the refrigerator box does not actually look like a complete rocket, but young children in particular communities come to see certain critical features of the box as being rocket enough to represent a vessel for space flight. This does not occur apart from cultural, social, or adult influence; however, we tend to see children's creation of this metaphor as both logical and innate. We do not have drills or workbooks related to boxes becoming modes of transportation. Similarly, our heads do not physically look like circles, but long before they enter formal schooling young children quickly come to use circles to depict heads in their drawings. In so doing they are creating a metaphor—"This shape will serve as a 'head.' It is headlike enough to convey my idea within my community."

Likewise, the emotion of joy is an internal feeling, but children give it symbolic shape in movements that adults often refer to as dance. Although dance may not look like the internal feeling of joy, it becomes its symbolic expression and thus gives joy a visible sign. Many very young children recognize the symbol of the *Golden Arches*, an ideogram, as representative of the McDonalds restaurant. In the same fashion, Sam's written name had come to depict him. He had come to associate critical features of himself with the written word *S-A-M*. The shape of the symbolized name (its form) contained the critical features Sam was seeking in how he metaphorically represented who he was to a surrounding world—a world, as Sam had come to realize, that embodied a great deal of meaning and importance in the simple, clustered, repeated shapes that make up written language. There exists no evidence that a child's initial forays into print are more intellectually taxing or more unnatural than the efforts to create signs from boxes, drawn figures, or dance. In each of a child's multiple sign systems, what appears necessary for developing sophistication is the presence of local understanding that allows for active symbolic participation and that takes seriously children's individual motivations in a responsive, literacy-rich context.

Initially, Sam's focus was on the beginning mark—*S*—and it mattered tremendously to him how the line curved. Not just any curved line would serve. Soon teachers would begin directing Sam in how to curve his line for an appropriate *S*, and as the mechanics of conformity take precedence, any understanding of the intellectual and emotional energy Sam once poured into his own sense of the curves will be lost. In his early efforts, if the *S* was not drawn specifically for his name, either by Sam or a teacher, Sam appeared not to associate the mark with a representation of himself. For instance, I observed a teacher's aide point to the *S* in the word stop and say to Sam, "Hey, *S* for *stop*, and *S* for Sam." Sam looked blankly at the word for a second and then said, "That's not me," and scooted off. At this point, Sam's sense of letters was still rigidly context specific. He was still *drawing words* rather than *drawing sounds*.

Although I argue that signs always remain contextually bound, we do develop the capacity to wrench a letter from one situation and carry it over to a new situation in order to construct meaning (and, of course, a new context for that letter). Conventional views of literacy suggest that printed language is inherently abstract and, therefore, can be moved from place to place and reconfigured as needed. Unfortunately, this view translates to how we teach young children about print. We begin with drills that are highly abstract and indeed purposefully stripped of meaning while ignoring that literacy begins and in many ways remains for the child a context bound endeavor. In a sense, the child is always saying, "How does this help me construct meaning right now?"

Four months after my initial observation, I again saw Sam sign his name. This time he was much quicker, and his signature involved three marks in a row from left to right. The first sign looked something like an *S* but it was not as intricately done as in my preceding observation. Sam was clearly developing a sense of linkage, sequence, linearity, and so forth. He was paying close attention to the number of marks clustered to form his name. Other children were commenting on the length of words, and to Sam's distress a degree of status had been bestowed on children with more marks making up their names.

I continued to observe Sam's printed efforts throughout the school year as well as the following school year when he was 4 years old, soon to be 5. There were moments when he spent a great deal of time writing his name in extremely clear fashion and other times when he reverted to a single mark. On other occasions, he wrote his name from right to left or with two letters instead of three. I also saw Sam sweep his finger across his name, sounding it out in slow fashion to suggest that he was learning that the graphemes he constructed represented words that could be spoken. Although there was a clear progression evident in his efforts, Sam demonstrated what I came to regard as a fairly typical nonlinear quality to literate development.

During an observation when Sam was nearly 5 years old, he walked over to me and said, "I need help." His intention was to create a sign for home that would keep his older siblings (i.e., "big kids" in Sam's parlance) out of his bedroom but allow his same-age friends (i.e., just "kids") to enter. "How do you write *kids allowed?*" he wanted to know.

I said, "It starts with *K*. You spell it *K-I-D-S*." Sam wrote the letters as I repeated them.

After he wrote the *K*, he asked, "Is this how you make a *K?*" He turned the paper toward me so that I was looking at it right side up. When he completed the word, he again turned the paper toward me and said, "Look," pointing to his zigzag-shaped *S*, "I made that *S* evil!" He laughed. I assumed then that his shape was accidental, and he ascribed meaning after the fact, but on the sign he drew a picture of "big kids" making their mouths in the exact shape of the *S*. "Look at!" he exclaimed. "They are evil." I never did learn why he thought of that shape as representative of evil, or what incident inspired the sign, but the interaction reminded me that it is important to be open to the possibility of intent in the actions of young children.

The Studies of Ashton-Warner and Freire

A child's name as well as a motivated phrase to hang on one's bedroom door are powerful and intimate words around which young children rally in their developing sophistication with signs and the complexities of printed language. Sylvia Ashton-Warner (1963) was a New Zealand educator who, in the middle decades of the 20th century, began to profoundly influence worldwide perceptions of young children's capacities to engage written language. She coined the term *organic reading*. In this frame, children's first written words "must mean something. First words must have intense meaning for a child. They must be part of his being" (p. 33). Ashton-Warner continued,

> How much hangs on the love of reading, the instinctive inclination to hold a book! *Instinctive.* That's what it must be. The reaching out for a book needs to become an organic action, which can happen at this yet formative [4- and 5-year-old children] age. Pleasant words won't do. Respectable words won't do. They must be words organically tied up, organically born from the dynamic life itself. They must be words that are already part of the child's being. (1963, p. 33)

Ashton-Warner was describing her initial literacy efforts with young Maori children, an indigenous, minority population in New Zealand. The Maori culture differed rather dramatically from the majority Eurocentric New Zealand culture, and the Maori children struggled in the majority-dominated school settings. This struggle was often cast in a racist light. Ashton-Warner, however, interpreted the struggle as a need to build bridges of literacy across cultural divides.

A central dimension of Ashton-Warner's literacy efforts was the development of children's key vocabularies. A child's key vocabulary in these cases was made up of words expressed by the child and noticed by the teacher to contain individual power or affective momentum. The teacher then wrote the key term on a large card and handed it to the child. In this sense (as well as many others), local understanding was central to literate development. The child had to be comfortable expressing emotional and affective ideas, and the teacher had to be capable of discerning those important terms on an individual basis. No two children shared the same key vocabulary; they were all highly individualized. Ashton-Warner described each word in a child's key vocabulary as a one-word narrative, a deceptively simple term chosen by the child to represent his or her inner state or condition. "They are more than captions," she wrote. "They are even more than sentences. They are whole stories at times. They are actually schematic drawing. I know because they tell them to me" (Ashton-Warner, 1963, p. 40). The children's key vocabularies were never sounded out by the child, but remembered as a unit whose shape was a metaphor for the embedded meaning.

As the Maori children built key vocabularies, they shared their cards with friends. Ashton-Warner (1963) wrote, "When they have collected their own cards they choose a partner and sit together and hear each other, their own and the other's words" (p. 47). She continued, "All this, of course, takes time and involves noise and movement and personal relations and actual reading, and above all communication, one with another: the vital thing so often cut off in a school" (p. 47). Here Ashton-Warner was noting the importance not just of literate representation, but literate communication as well! Together the children taught one another.

From key vocabularies in Ashton-Warner's (1963) classrooms, children began to "organically" (p. 51) write stories. Initially these were often the single-word key terms integrally embedded in drawings that told the child's tale. "The creative writing of fives [5-year-old children] begins with their attempts to write their own key words, and since they have found out that these scrawly shapes mean something, they know what they are writing about more than I do" (p. 51). She continued,

> From here they join in with the stream of autobiographical writing.... Fives have a most distinctive style. And they write these sentences of the same pattern with its varied content so often that they learn automatically the repeated words and consolidate their style—with scarcely any teaching from me, which transfers the whole question of spelling, word study and composition into the vent of creativity. (1963, pp. 51–52)

Ashton-Warner's deep sense that literacy grows out of the symbolic presence and narrative experiences of the children themselves is shared with Paulo Freire, another extremely influential educator of the 20th century. Freire, with his colleague Macedo, (1987) noted that "Reading the world always precedes reading the word" (p. 29), which means that children's experiences should serve as the basis of literacy. At times "reading the world" is misconstrued as requiring that young children's stories be concrete or reality based. Instead, we must remember that children's worlds are heavily adorned with, and influenced by, fantasy, magic, monsters, superheroes, and other metaphysical forms. Based on experience, Freire (1970/1993) pointed out, students—both children and adults—can begin the literate act of naming the world, which is a transformative act. "To exist humanly," Freire insisted, "is to name the world, to change it" (p. 69).

Freire's initial efforts with the literate *naming of the world* occurred in the 1960s among the impoverished and oppressed people of northeast Brazil, Freire's native country (see Freire, 1970/1993). With support from the Ministry of Education, Freire and his literacy fieldworkers devised dialogues that opened up reflective introspection among the poor and desolate population regarding the oppression they were experiencing. As with the life experiences of Ashton-Warner's Maori students serving as the basis for their early literacy, the reflective dialogues initiated by Freire—around land, work, nutrition, health care, and so forth—provided the initial sources of writing for the Brazilian peasants. Instruction in writing was organically tied to their world, and literacy flowed forth into a massive social justice movement. With written language, those who had been subjugated suddenly saw themselves as having a voice and a right to economic justice. Unfortunately, a right wing military coup toppled the Brazilian government in 1964, and Freire was immediately jailed. After several months in prison he was sent into exile.

Both Ashton-Warner and Freire noted how their literacy methods sharply contrasted with the imposed, monotonous, mechanistic approaches that dominated the day and remain shockingly prevalent in the opening years of the 21st century. Ashton-Warner (1963) pointed out that in other early childhood classrooms the adult "educationists" chose the children's vocabulary. She noted that a programmed reader published in America informed teachers that "A child can be led to feel that Janet and John are friends" (p. 33). In italicized print Ashton-Warner cried, *"Can be led to feel.* Why lead the child to feel or try to lead him to feel that these strangers are friends? What about the passionate feeling he has already for his own friends?" (p. 33). About the key vocabulary, Ashton-Warner pointed out, "It is an opportune moment to observe the emotional distance of these private vocabularies from the opening words of the 'Janet and John' book: *Janet John come look and see boats little dog run here down up...."*(p. 44). In contrast, her 5-year-olds were writing stories about joy and despair. One of these children wrote, "I went to the river and I kissed Lily and I ran away. Then I kissed Phillica. Then I ran away and went for a swim," (p. 53). Another scrawled, "Mummie got a hiding off Daddy. He was drunk she was crying" (p. 53).

Freire (1970/1993) described in critical fashion traditional didactic educational methods as a banking concept where students are the depositories and the teacher is the depositor. Freire argued, "In the banking concept of education, knowledge is a gift bestowed by those who consider themselves knowledgeable upon those whom they consider to know nothing" (p. 53). He continued, "Projecting an absolute ignorance onto others, a characteristic of the ideology of oppression, negates inquiry and knowledge as processes of education" (p. 53). In Freire's mind, true inquiry is essential to true education. Furthermore, the student and teacher must not be seen as oppositional poles, but each must be constantly seen as the other—the student as teacher and the teacher as student. Similarly, Ashton-Warner (1963) explained that the children taught her how to teach them to read. "There is no force to marshal the children into an attentive group," she explained (p. 50), "The teaching is done among themselves, mixed up with all the natural concomitants of relationship" (p. 51). She is, of course, describing 4- and 5-year-old children.

Multiple Sign Systems

Young children's literacy is a flow that churns forth from their symbolic presence, constructed narratives, and crafted signs. On entering preschool, young children are already experts at using a range of symbolic sign systems in interactive fashion to make sense of their world. Children never work within a single sign system; rather, they constantly combine forms and modes in their construction of meaning. Kress (1997) refers to this fluidity as *synaesthesia* (p. 39) or the translation and transduction of meaning across multiple symbolic modes. Symbolic modes in the inclusive early childhood classroom may include, among an infinite array of others, the signs and symbols of fantasy and dramatic play; formal and informal curricula; computer keyboards, text, animation, and icons appearing on screen and printed; materials associated with board games and puzzles; pictures, symbols, and text on clothing and hats; hallway signs; posted materials targeting parents; music (both child initiated and adult directed); dance and other movements associated with music, song, and chants; poetry read, recited, chanted, and created; Popsicle stick art; American Sign Language and signed English; and so forth.

In 1983, neuroscientist Howard Gardner famously proposed a theory of multiple intelligences to more adequately represent human intellect than was accomplished by traditional models of a general intelligence. Gardner (1991) noted that of the eight intelligences he has identified, "each is susceptible to capture in a symbolic or notational system" (p. 81). Within the linguistic intelligence, one of the eight, Gardner pointed out that children come to master the syntax of their native language and also to develop the capacity to construct narratives across genres and with varying degrees of complexity. Within musical intelligence, another of the eight, children quickly discover the organization of tonal pitch structures and their representation through sound and notation. This, Gardner suggested, reflects the *syntax* of music, expanding the traditional meaning of the term.

Gardner described these syntactical systems as occurring in streams of symbolic development, but with each symbol stream and its

growth remaining quite separate from the other streams. "It is my conclusion," Gardner (1991) explained, "that one syntactic trajectory has
no close relation to other syntactic trajectories" (p. 74). Gardner's spec-
ulation would seem to contradict my assertion that the sign systems of
early childhood are recursive and interlinked. I agree that competence
in one area does not develop wholly because competence develops in
other areas. For instance, in a hypothetical population absent forms of
music, the development of alphabetic skills will not elicit musical competence. If there is no opportunity to actively engage a particular sign
system, whether it is spoken language, dance, or written language, the
child will not develop in that area. Responding to the apparent contra-
diction, however, Gardner (1991) himself went on to explain that for
the preschool child, "syntactic capacities [using his broadened sense of
the term], the building blocks of cognition, abound. The child tells stories, counts objects, makes drawings, and begins to devise notations"
(p. 82). He continued,

> The child is attempting to make overall sense of the world; she is seeking
> to integrate the waves, streams, and channels of her own complex of intel-
> ligences into a comprehensive version of human life.... She is strongly
> constrained to carry out this integration, for survival could not take place
> in the absence of some coherent version of the world. (1991, p. 83)

Thus, Gardner's separate sign systems do become integrated in
the child's effort to build a coherent picture of the surrounding world.
In addition, research has demonstrated that if one particular sign-
based system for the socially driven construction of meaning is absent,
children will shift to other systems, which suggests their interactivity
and interdependence. For instance, infants who are born deaf and who
are exposed to sign language will not babble vocally but will "babble"
with their hands. Infants who are born deaf who are not exposed to
sign, however, do not babble vocally or with their hands (Petitto &
Marentette, 1991).

Babbling is the unfortunate term applied to infants' diligent and
systematic inclination and effort to begin building social connections
and constructs of meaning through the symbols of language. In their
babbling, babies are recreating the rudimentary structures, rhythms,
and patterns of the language surrounding them, which results in
infants babbling in particular vocal patterns and rhythms. Petitto and
Marentette (1991) found that infants who are deaf and exposed to a rich
environment of sign begin to form the rhythms and patterns of sign
language as they attempt to build social connections and make sense of
the world. Petitto and Marentette's study demonstrated that when a
physical difference acts as an obstacle to engaging in spoken language

(considered the natural or normal first sign system), children do not simply stagnate but make use of other *natural* sign systems to construct meaning.

In addition, research has demonstrated that vocal babbling on the part of hearing infants is not just a product of auditory engagement, but that it also involves intense visual concentration on the part of infants who watch the lips, facial characteristics, and muscle motor movements of surrounding speakers (Weikum et al., 2007). Weikum and colleagues (2007) found that at 4 months, babies were able to distinguish between facial movements, absent the sound, associated with different languages! This illustrates that characteristics so closely connected to the aural may also be fundamentally visual. That said, I should point out that infants who are born blind quickly babble and develop speech, so they, too, must have paths that allow for the circumvention of the predominant or majority routes (those termed *normal*) to language development.

My research supports the view that the various sign systems, when thoughtfully engaged, may recursively and transcursively foster the developing complexities of other sign systems. For instance, a vast array of evidence indicates that providing young children who are not developing speech with alternative or augmentative communication systems (e.g., sign language, communication icons) actually fosters the development of speech in many children (Mirenda, 2003). Furthermore, in any sign system (dance, drawing, alphabetic print, fantasy play, and so forth), the child is learning to make visible in metaphor and symbol his or her symbolic presence through the expression of narratives. He or she also is learning to garner information from the symbols of others. The philosopher and linguist Bakhtin (1986) described a text as "any coherent complex of signs...even the study of art deals with texts" (p. 103). Gallas agreed, noting,

> I realized that the practice of carefully reading pictures is essential for the mastery of many subjects at higher levels. For example, when we look at a painting, we are reading a text; when studying biology, we read the slides under the microscope; we learn to read maps, graphs, music, and equations. (2003, p. 20)

Unfortunately, most early literacy programs ignore children's synaesthesic capacities. These programs yank from children their proclivity to construct meaning through multiple sign systems based on the erroneous sense that anything other than formal written language is extraneous and distracting to the real intellectual work of schooling. This needlessly reduces children's opportunities and in fact may close symbol-based doors of access to printed language. Certain children's routes to writing may require extended forays through, for example, drawing, acting, or musical composition. When denied these paths, certain children may struggle with symbolic representation. When a child struggles, the literacy program is rarely blamed or found to be in disorder; rather, we ascribe disorder to the brain of the child in question.

THE TENUOUS RELATIONSHIP BETWEEN THE CHILD AND LITERATE CITIZENSHIP

The importance of the symbolic presence, narrative construction, and development of sign systems to a young child's literate citizenship emerged in my research as I studied environments where local understanding made visible that which has historically and conventionally been rendered invisible in relation to children with significant developmental disabilities. Early childhood special education personnel have largely addressed young children with significant developmental disabilities as though they lack the capacity to construct meaning, imagine, develop a symbolic connectedness with others, craft narratives of any genre, and actively construct signs in a critical fashion.

Common to nearly all young children who have moderate to severe disabilities, including in my studies, is a profound struggle with communication generally and speech specifically. As noted previously, Vygotsky and those who followed have emphasized speech as central to the child's construction of meaning. When a child's expressions are poorly understood or entirely missed by people in positions of relative authority (e.g., educators), the child is invariably the one blamed (so to speak) and he or she is labeled as having cognitive, linguistic, social, and communicative disabilities.

The privileging of speech in conjunction with labeling a child with disabilities acts to render invisible the literate citizenship and potential of young children with limited speech. This frequently occurs due to segregation of children labeled with disabilities by special education professionals (for critical discussions, see Katims, 2000; Kliewer & Biklen, 2001; Kliewer, Biklen, & Kasa-Hendrickson, 2006; Mirenda, 2003). As described in Chapter 1, Isaac briefly experienced this invisibility of a symbolic self when he was, as his mother phrased it, turned into "nothing but a defect" in the segregated special education classroom devoid of literate opportunities.

Similarly, I encountered an example of invisibility in a research interview conducted with a teacher in a segregated school for students with significant disabilities. The teacher explained that 2 years earlier she had chosen to work with 5- and 6-year-old children in the segregated special education job rather than in a first-grade position in a general education school in the same small city because, as the teacher explained, "In first grade here [the city's school system] there is so much pressure to teach reading. It's make or break. You have so many people watching, and the pressure is intense. Here [the segregated special education school] there's no teaching reading. I don't have to worry about it. My kids aren't readers and they never will be. They'll never write. They don't even have any language."

Both the social and psychological models of literacy (i.e., outside in or inside out) present a flawed sense of a mechanistic literate arena into which children are said to move. Children with significant developmental disabilities, however, are commonly cast as wholly incapable of constructing meaning in such a stable, symbolic realm. In rather straightforward fashion, this teacher disavowed any possibility or visibility of literate citizenship on the part of her segregated students. This invisibility translated into the absence of opportunities for literacy in the classroom. The segregated school in which this teacher taught included no student library, and the classrooms commonly lacked any normal child-oriented reading materials, such as storybooks. It would be difficult to be anything but subliterate surrounded by such disconnection from written opportunities.

The daily literate invisibility experienced directly by each student in this segregated school was affirmed and shaped by an abstract invisibility. By this I mean the establishment of categorical rules by professional expert authorities. The abstract category is used as the framework to set the contours of possibility for the actual individual. This individual, who is interpreted as wholly incompetent, is then used to affirm the category. Thus, the limitations of the abstract are presumed to be the limitations of the actual, and the actual is only known through a categorical lens of utter hopelessness that obscures or makes invisible the actuality or possibility of literate citizenship.

In contrast to convention, environments organized around local understanding promote the visibility of every child's symbolic presence, narrative formation, and sign use. In effect, the stance is taken that all citizens have something to say even if they are difficult to comprehend and their meaning is obscure. When literacy is understood to be transformed, crafted, and created by children in action, the notion of literate brokenness makes no sense. Children are crafting meaning from a particular vantage point that makes sense to them at that moment. The teacher's role is to prod, pull, coax, and foster connections of increasingly sophisticated, symbolic meaning across children. There is never a preliterate stage in a child's life. Rather, the forms of the child's symbolic presence, narrative, and sign construction are constantly changing.

The development of a symbolic tapestry begins in inclusive environments with every child recognized as a rightful and valued citizen. For instance, in Chapter 3, Joey, a child with complex needs on the autism spectrum, was initially described as a child who bit others when he became upset. However, as difficult as this behavior was to Joey's citizenship, it did not suggest to the surrounding adults that he did not belong. "Where would we send him?" Ms. Perry asked in response to a question on whether Joey's biting might be cause for removal from the program. Instead of removing Joey, the teachers interpreted his biting as a form of communication. "He was telling us something and we weren't listening—yet," she said. Increased adult supports were added as well as a focus on developing a communication system that was understandable and efficient. That, in combination with a room full of peers who did not communicate through biting, rendered Joey's biting a distant memory by the end of the school year.

Shirley Kehoe, lead teacher of the inclusive Prairie View public preschool program, told me early one morning before her 17 students arrived,

> Literacy is about storytelling. You have got to get the kids telling stories. Everything is storytelling. You make a list—you're telling the story of your day. The schedule for instance, that's a story of our day. The list is the story of your grocery shopping.

Ms. Kehoe was suggesting that even something as seemingly rudimentary and utilitarian as a list fit the definition of narrative in that it contained an embedded subject with a perspective (e.g., a child, the group as a whole, the teacher), an understandable structure, and a tacit affective force (e.g., this is what we want, this is what we need, this is how we will accomplish our wants and needs).

Ms. Kehoe further explained that merely being exposed to storytelling was not enough. Children needed to be actively participating.

> But you need to see yourself as a storyteller, and a lot of kids have gotten the message, 'You don't have anything to say.' And they've gotten no chance or opportunity to say it! They're shut out of the conversation.

Here Ms. Kehoe was explicitly referring to children with significant developmental disabilities.

Young children's symbolic presence, narratives, and sign systems are dynamic and teeming with metaphor. Thus, literacy requires someone capable of these characteristics. In contrast, significant disability (and the young child so labeled) is culturally constructed as *static*—simple, one-dimensional, dormant, stalled, and fossilized. A child with significant developmental disabilities is culturally constructed in a calcifying vein as "something static, something beheld from afar, not complex, not shifting in meaning" (Biklen, 2000, p. 339). Disability becomes an idea that precludes the possibility of dynamism, metaphor, and symbolism, one that precludes the possibility of literate citizenship.

Larry Bissonnette spent much of his life interpreted through the static lens of disability. Now in his forties, Bissonnette expresses rich, recognized narratives through his critically acclaimed art that mixes drawing, painting, and photography (Biklen & Rosetti, 2005; Bissonnette, 2005). Originally labeled with autism and significant intellectual disabilities, Bissonnette spent his formative years locked in the Brandon State Training School, a decrepit institution for people classified as having severe intellectual disabilities. Bissonnette's spoken language is often nonsensical, repetitive, echolalic, and explosively impulsive. He types on a keyboard to communicate. Initially his typing was physically facilitated, but he now is able to type with minimal support. He noted, "I rely on typing for my personally important ideas" (Biklen & Rosetti, 2005).

Bissonnette's journey from institution inmate to artist began when his sister, Sally Veraway, visited him in the institution. In a documentary, she recalled, "I saw Larry in awful condition—all medicated, sitting on the floor, legs crossed, banging his head on the wall" (Biklen & Rosetti, 2005). A static interpretation of significant disability commonly suggests this is simply a mirror of the category, an apt reflection of how things are and how they must be. Veraway, however, brought local insight to the horrific scene. With the assistance of a small group of people that would eventually include, among others, an art teacher and an employee of a community-based disability support organization, Bissonnette was freed from the institution and joined the wider community where he became an artist.

Veraway noted that her brother had always been capable of crafting complex narratives in a variety of sign systems but that these efforts had been rendered invisible in the institution. She recalled,

> [Larry] used to get up in the middle of the night, sneak into the kitchen, steal a butter knife, pick a lock, go into the sewing room, take all their brand new sheets at the Brandon Training School and make curtains. He sewed them by hand. (Biklen & Rosetti, 2005)

Veraway was, of course, pointing out the complexity and imagination inherent in Bissonnette's narrative sequence. Personnel at the institution used the same patterns to reduce Bissonnette to a troublemaker and rule breaker. Indeed, institutional definitions of autism list impaired imagination as a symptom (e.g., APA, 2004). Defining an individual as organically lacking an imagination is dehumanizing and precludes literate citizenship. When asked how some are able to see him as an artist while others only see disability, Bissonnette typed out that those who held a local understanding are "less worried about Larry's peculiarities and more attuned to my potential" (Biklen & Rosetti, 2005).

How would Bissonnette's life have been different if literate possibilities had been opened to him from his toddler days? Would it have been different if a paint brush and oils had been provided in a rich inclusive preschool rather than his actual experience of being thrust behind locked doors at Brandon State Training School? Yet, while reliance on institutions has dwindled, young children with significant developmental disabilities continue to face mass preschool segregation and highly restrictive access to a generally thoughtless form of literacy. In a previous study, I noted that often the only literacy provided to a child with trisomy 21, autism, cerebral palsy, or another developmental disability (when any is provided at all) comes in the form of a limited set of Mayer-Johnson or Bliss symbols chosen by adults and arranged for the child on a laminated communication board (Kliewer & Biklen, 2001). These boards might include extremely abstract, line-drawn, two-dimensional symbols indicating words and phrases such as *eat, bathroom, yes, no,* and *all done.* A misguided assumption is that these symbols are somehow more concrete than the written word.

Certainly the communication boards, when used, depict important words, but by definition these are not the words erupting from the life-worlds of the children. As described in more detail in the next chapter, adult-chosen symbols do not reflect the passion of young children. They do not explode from the child but are imposed from on high. The assumption, of course, is that these children labeled with significant developmental disabilities have no stories to express. This is the core belief that must be toppled in our local drive to support the citizenship of all children in the literate community.

Chapter 5

"And I Looked in Those Eyes"

Fostering the Literate Citizenship of Young Children with Significant Developmental Disabilities

In autobiographical research articles, presentations, a video documentary, and even a CNN feature and *People* magazine spread, Jamie Burke, a young man with autism and now a student at Syracuse University, openly discusses his literacy-based, typed communication as a 4-year-old in an inclusive preschool (Biklen & Burke, 2006; Burke, 2005, 2007; Fields-Meyer, Duffy, & Arias, 2005; Kasa-Hendrickson, Broderick, & Biklen, 2002). While in the preschool, Burke, unable then to make himself understood through spoken language, recalled typing the phrase "to loud" (mistake in the original typing). His preschool teacher had approached him with a small keyboard and asked, "Why are you so upset, Jamie?" (Burke, 2007). He was telling her through a typed two-word phrase that the classroom at that moment was too loud for his comfort.

Burke's vocal language at that time was seemingly dysfunctional and highly echolalic. His scores on developmental assessments suggested profound cognitive delays. Personnel at his inclusive preschool, however, administered the assessments largely out of bureaucratic necessity and never felt the low scores presented an accurate or honest picture of the young child's gifts and competencies. This was a school built on local understanding in which teachers focused on seeing Burke's full and rightful citizenship.

In the hectic preschool classroom, Burke has recalled gravitating toward the quiet stability of the library corner where teachers noticed him avidly devouring books, sometimes with two open at once. Similar to Lori, the 4-year-old at Bethel Nursery School (see Chapter 3), typing on a Dynavox, Burke appeared drawn to printed language. Rather than dismissing his interest as irrelevant or even an obsession or compulsion, school personnel began to systematically support his use of printed language for communicative purposes.

Similar to how Joey was described in Chapter 3 as choosing words and symbols to co-construct a note home and based on principles inspired by Ashton-Warner (as described in Chapter 4), Burke's initial efforts with the alphabet were structured around choosing prewritten words as captions for high-interest photos of family, friends, and home life or other such depictions of his experiences. Ashton-Warner (1963) used what she referred to as the interior pictures from the children's minds expressed through speech. For Burke, whose speech was limited and very difficult to decipher, teachers needed to develop an alternative. Initially the captions to the photos were choices created by the teacher on separate cards. For example, asking, "Is this a photo of *Mom* or *Dad*, Jamie?" would prompt Burke to point to the prewritten word. Within the span of a few weeks, Burke was sequencing letters into words using a letterboard, keyboard, or a small typing device made by Canon called a Communicator. Within another few weeks—all at the age of 4 years—he was typing two- and three-word sentences.

Since the mid-1990s, a heightened scientific interest has emerged in the centrality of kinesthetic dilemmas experienced by people with autism and other developmental disabilities (Bauman & Kemper, 1995). Recent definitions of autism recognize that these individuals have complex motor planning difficulties that profoundly inhibit the initiation and continuance of what would normally be volitional movements (Donnellan & Leary, 1995). Burke's awkward, jilting actions demonstrated these struggles. Because of this, his teachers never introduced, nor did he naturally gravitate toward, conventional crayon writing. Rather, Burke's teachers moved directly to supporting his use of a finger to point to words and then to type on a keyboard, actions that require less dexterity than needed for effective use of crayons or markers on a blank page. Even the simple movement of a finger extending proved complex for the preschooler, and a keyguard was placed over the keyboard. In addition, similar to the teacher assisting Joey to craft the note home and the typing effort of Larry Bissonnette (see Chapter 4), an adult gave physical support (or facilitation) to Burke's hand to allow him to maintain a pointer finger, cue his movement forward, and sustain his typing motion once initiated.

THE STRUGGLE FOR LITERATE ACCEPTANCE

Over the course of several years, during which he naturally garnered countless hours of typing practice, Burke's capacity to control his volitional movements improved to the point where he now types independently and with two hands. Burke is what language researcher Pat Mirenda (2003) describes as one of a "growing number of individuals in North America and elsewhere who once relied on facilitation (i.e., physical support of the hand or arm and emotional support) to type but are now independent typists or even functional speakers" (p. 273). At age 4, however, pointing without physical support was still an impossibility for Burke. The combination of necessary facilitation from an adult, Burke's tender age, and the idea of a child with significant developmental disabilities constructing even simple typed words combined to draw a degree of incredulity directed at Burke's communication. The question arose, "Are his teachers who physically support his typing inadvertently cuing or even directing his typing?"

The question is a variation of the often virulent skepticism historically directed at the literate success of individuals with significant disabilities who, according to convention, are hopelessly aliterate. For instance, most of us are aware of the story of Anne Sullivan, who has been described as a miracle worker for leading her young student, Helen Keller, into language. Following a fever in infancy, Keller lost her hearing, sight, and, according to most people around her at the time, her potential capacity to think and reason. Her extended family pressured her mother to institutionalize her. Instead, her parents sought out Sullivan to be her teacher. Keller, according to the miracle worker tale, proved to be a daunting, but ultimately successful, student who went from the fabled moment at the water pump to a full life of scholarship and activism.

Left out of the miracle worker folklore, however, was a deeply troubling side to the tale. As Keller and Sullivan gained recognition for their accomplishments, the majority of educational professionals who at the time were working with deaf or blind children declared Keller to be a hoax and accused Sullivan of perpetrating a fraud. The director of Boston's Perkins School for the Blind (for which Sullivan initially worked), Michael Anagnos, publicly stated, "Helen Keller is a living lie" (quoted in Lash, 1980, p. 168).

The accusations arose because Keller was said to be literate beyond what was considered possible for someone who was both deaf and blind. Explained Alexander Johnson, General Secretary of the National Conference on Charities and Corrections and a contemporary of Keller's:

The chronic insane, the epileptic, the paralytic, the imbecile and idiot of various grades, the moral imbecile, the sexual pervert ... *the blind, deaf-mutes.* All these classes in varying degrees with others not mentioned, are related as being degenerates. (1903, p. 246, emphasis added)

According to definition and convention, an individual so insensitively labeled *degenerate* could not function as a full and literate citizen of society. The skepticism directed at Keller's literate citizenship would follow her throughout her illustrious life. The psychologist Thomas D. Cutsforth (1933) wrote in *The Blind in School and Society: A Psychological Study* that Keller's writings reflected "implied chicanery" (p. 48). A *New York Nation* review of Keller's autobiography described her writing as "lacking in literary veracity" and rife with "literary insincerity" (as quoted in Braddy, 1933, p. 201).

As an adult, Keller grew exhausted trying to continuously prove her competence. She ultimately responded that those who raised doubts about her capacity bore the burden of proof. It was not, Keller argued, her obligation to continuously validate her abilities (Einhorn, 1998). Keller stated,

Some brave doubters have even gone so far even as to deny my existence. In order, therefore, that I may know that I exist, I resort to Descartes' method: "I think therefore I am." Thus I am metaphysically established, and I throw upon the doubters the burden of proving my nonexistence. (1920, p. 40)

In a 1908 magazine article, Keller wrote,

Has anything arisen to disprove the adequacy of my correspondence? Has any chamber of the blind man's brain been opened and found empty? Has any psychologist explored the mind of the sightless and been able to say, "There is no sensation here"? When we consider how little has been found out about the mind, is it not amazing that anyone should presume to define what one can know or cannot know? (1908, p. 782)

As did Keller in the previous century, Burke now expresses frustration with those who, because of his disability, reject his capacity to construct symbolic, literate meaning of the surrounding world. He explained, "I felt so mad as [certain] teachers spoke in their childish voices to me, mothering me but not educating me" (Biklen & Burke, 2006, p. 169). Burke continued,

I understand why kids scream. It's frustrating not being able to speak and feeling as a mostly invisible being. Do you know the vintage movie, *The Invisible Man*? That's how I felt. My clothes were there but the body and soul felt like nothing. How can you live a life getting treated like that? (2006, p. 171).

REALIZING A LITERATE VOICE

Burke's preschool teachers who introduced him to literacy-based communication recognized that the developmental assessments and tests they were bureaucratically required to administer merely reflected how Burke's growth failed to follow the trajectory of the majority. His autism label already suggested his path was distinct from that taken by most children. Because of his severe struggles with movement planning, Burke did not easily demonstrate the actions (and, of course, spoken language) associated with young children's dramatic and fantasy play. He did not move easily to the easel or art center to pick up paint brushes and crayons to make the first marks of what would become written language. In short, he was not going to take the majority path (referred to as *developmentally appropriate*) from playing to drawing to writing. In the environment of local understanding, however, Burke's teachers recognized that he was no less driven to construct symbolic meaning of his surrounding world than were his typically developing peers.

In Chapter 4, I described certain language studies that demonstrated that deaf infants brought up in sign language environments quickly began to recreate the patterns and rhythms of sign just as hearing infants recreate the patterns and rhythms of spoken language (Petitto & Marentette, 1991). When the majority route to language is somehow impeded for particular children, their symbolic presence does not merely languish; rather, children appear to actively alter the manner through which they construct narratives and sign systems. Deaf infants adjusted to sign.

For Burke, who was labeled as a child with autism, his spoken language proved deeply ineffective. Sign language, which is kinesthetically less complex than the motor patterns required for the physical production of speech, may have served Burke as an alternative, but he was not brought up in an environment that used American Sign Language (ASL). Furthermore, his difficulties with volitional movement probably would have required that his signing be physically facilitated for some time just as his typing needed to be.

Burke was, however, brought up in a print-rich home and traveled through a print-rich community to arrive every morning at a print-rich inclusive preschool. Whereas his typically developing peers' communicative energy was largely and quite naturally directed toward an emphasis on spoken language, Burke appeared drawn to print. When his teachers showed Burke how he might make use of written language to interactively communicate thought and spirit and socially construct meaning, Burke's syntactical and orthographic capacities appeared to explode—similar to seeing moments of dramatic spurts in the spoken language development of typically developing children and the sign language development of deaf children.

Other researchers have found a similar, seemingly startling or even counterintuitive skill with, and perhaps comfort in, printed language among very young children with significant developmental disabilities commonly linked to communication and cognitive delays. British language scientist Susan Buckley, for instance, has spent nearly 3 decades developing the literate profiles of preschoolers with trisomy 21 (Down syndrome) (e.g., Buckley, 1984; Buckley, 2006). Her work describes dozens of toddlers and preschool children, all of whom have been identified as having moderate to severe cognitive delays, and some as young as 2 years, learning to read alphabetic print at levels far beyond what is generally conceived to be possible for typically developing preschool children. Similar to autism, trisomy 21 is closely associated with motor planning difficulties, although these difficulties have largely and unfortunately been ignored as extraneous and peripheral to the supposed core dilemmas associated with the chromosomal anomaly.

Buckley (2006) pointed out that her young research participants, much like Burke, were learning to read prior to demonstrating recognizable or seemingly useful spoken language. Conventional attitudes about literacy largely disregard children's early efforts with visual, orthographic, and tactile sign systems. Formal literacy programs that grow out of conventional ideas focus solely on children's orthographic expressions and only begin after speech is well developed. Emphasis and primacy is placed on spoken language in the early years of a child's life, whereas written language is considered a secondary lexicographic effort that begins only when teachers impose drill and regimen in a child's literate experiences. First, according to this framework, a child learns to talk, and then a child is made aware through direct teacher instruction that talk is made up of strings of sound that can be analyzed and ultimately represented by simple shapes strung together.

In contrast to conventional ideas about literacy, Buckley (2006) noted that young children with trisomy 21 were not learning to read as a secondary system but as a first language (much as spoken language is considered to be the first language of typically developing children). Rather than following the three stages that begin with seeing the printed word (patterned letters and graphemes that form morphemes), translating the printed word into its spoken form (phonemes, either out loud or silently), and finally comprehending the word, the young children involved in her studies were going straight from seeing the printed word to deciphering its meaning without translating it first into speech (just as children who speak go straight from speech to meaning). Evidence of this first occurred when certain of Buckley's preschool research participants who had the ability to articulate one-word utterances demonstrated *logical* semantic errors when reading flashcards. For instance, when shown the word *shut*, a 3-year-old child said, "Closed." When shown the word *ship*, a child said, "Boat." These children were going straight from the visual image of the word to its meaning.

Among the countless literate efforts engaged in prior to formal school-based reading programs, young children discover in different ways and at different paces that writing involves *drawing sounds*. What distinguishes this from certain other prominent preschool efforts with two-dimensional symbols is that the child is not trying to make the sign look in a physical way like the meaning he or she is trying to capture. Meaning and form are not obviously integral.

Of course, this separation from realism occurs in other sign systems as well. For instance, I observed a 3-year, 10-month-old child scribble frenetically over a drawing in red marker. She held it up and said, "Her is really mad." The red was definitely a sign, form and meaning interlinked, for anger that did not look like anger so much as it felt like anger. Another child might represent anger in the form of slanted eyebrows to show a mad face, which attempts to physically capture the look of ire or hostility. As such, children are constantly shifting among sign systems—some grounded in realism and some not—to represent aspects of narratives.

In terms of *drawing sound*, formal programs for beginning readers focus exclusively on this sound-to-letter link but in a manner that eliminates the *drawing* (or creative act) and replaces it with drill, worksheets, and stickers of praise or teacher marks in red ink indicating error. Buckley's young participants emphasize that *drawing sound* may be one aspect of developing alphabetic literacy for perhaps many children, but it is not the singular identifier of beginning reading and writing. Furthermore, for children whose speech is not recognized as useful by the surrounding world, realizing some connection between speech and writing may be necessary to open the floodgates of language (in this case written). However, the children may quickly come to see the symbols of written language as having a particular logic unto themselves without requiring speech, just as typically developing children realize the logic of strung-together sounds without requiring letters, graphemes, and morphemes.

With regard to the first language/second language example used previously, when learning a foreign language, people begin by translating a word from their first language into its closest equivalent in the second language. In the same way, when hearing a word in a second language, people initially translate it into the first language equivalent and then arrive at its meaning (e.g., from *arbre* in French to *tree* to an internal image of a tree). As fluency develops, however, this cumbersome need to translate dissipates by degree until no translation is necessary, and the individual is said to be able to *think* in the second language. Young children particularly have demonstrated remarkable proficiency in this capacity to fluently take on second and even third languages.

Again, for the young child with moderate to severe developmental disabilities, there may be some necessity to understand the existence of a link between speech and writing, but the child should not be forced to remain stuck at this point while surrounding adults await the emergence of traditional phonemic awareness indicators from the child. Rather, the child should be supported in his or her symbolic presence, narrative construction, and crafting of visual, orthographic, and tactile signs rather than demanding these efforts always be linked to spoken language.

CURRENTS OF LITERATE CITIZENSHIP

Children's transformational capacities as literate citizens are built on local understanding and are directly fostered in inclusive early childhood programs through what I describe as *currents of literacy.* The four currents I have identified are as follows:

1. Making sense of the sign-based narratives of others
2. Finding and expressing meaning in one's own experience through narratives crafted from visual, orthographic, and tactile sign systems
3. Developing complexity with visual, orthographic, or tactile sign systems in sustaining or generating narratives
4. Deriving joy and other affective forces from critical, reflective engagement with visual, orthographic, and tactile sign systems

These four currents allow the young child to begin constructing and transforming the visual, orthographic, and tactile sign systems associated with literacy. They foster the developing capacity to

- Construct and interpret metaphors
- Link meaning and form to craft signs in two and three dimensions
- Develop understanding that signs, whether visual, orthographic, or tactile, can assist in representing and communicating reality and fantasy or fact and fiction

- Translate signs from three dimensions to two (and back again)

- Understand that in two dimensions one expresses on a particular surface and as such must make decisions about how to construct that space using various media and employing particular designs that may strive to visually reproduce reality (e.g., a picture) or represent a symbol in place of realism

- Recognize at some level that drawing two-dimensional letters of the alphabet is a form of drawing sound

- Realize that text is important

- Understand that text contains meaning

- Comprehend that groups of letters that are clustered and arranged from left to right are purposefully patterned and can convey information or be meaningfully deciphered

- Realize that particular repeatable, relatively simple shapes can capture the complexities of thought and emotion

- Develop the orthographic sense that certain important elements (including sound) are attached to particular letters and arrangements of letters

- Conclude that text occurs in lines or organized blocks

- Recognize that writing is organized visually and set in space, unlike speech, which has a short-lived existence

- Realize that complex clauses from main to subordinate may be layered and retrieved through written language so that complex ideas and stories may be told

- Construct the sense that marks that are closely connected or linked have meaning

- Recognize that written language has spatial qualities, layout, and directionality

- See that written language is often linear

- Realize that patterns of letters and individual letters may be removed from one situation and moved to a new situation to create new form and meaning

- Begin to recognize patterns of letters as actual, interpretable words

The following section illustrates and expounds on local understanding and its embedded currents and how they might be a part of young children's literate lives.

The Sunshine Room Restaurant

Down the hall from Isaac's Corner Nook classroom at the inclusive Shoshone School was the Sunshine Room made up of 17 children 4 years old or just turning 5. During one afternoon observation, I stumbled into a pretend play restaurant scene as it unfolded. In the center of a play area, teacher Stacie Marks had arranged several tables (many of which were cube-shaped plastic chairs tipped on their side) with salt shakers, plastic utensils, and various menus collected from local establishments. Off to the side was a play kitchen area available to the children year round.

Several children sat at the tables pouring over the menus and shouting out orders to the waiter, Tristian, a 4-year-old wearing an oversize apron who scribbled on a pad and exhibited tremendous control over his customers.

"I want the psss-ghetti," one student yelled with his menu open to a page with a photo of ziti and sauce.

Tristian leaned over the boy and, with seemingly great care, made marks similar to the letter Z. Suddenly, he retorted, "You get the pizza," and his careful markings devolved into furious scribbles.

"How much is my supper?" a student asked the waiter, grabbing a stack of fake money.

"Eight hundred dollars," the waiter responded.

"I don't have eight hundred dollars," the patron replied.

"Then you're out of the restaurant!" the waiter yelled.

"I don't have eight hundred dollars either," another customer said.

"Then you're kicked out, too," the waiter responded.

As the drama unfolded, I watched Benson lying on his stomach and propped on a pillow at the periphery of the play area where an adult had positioned him amid a variety of percussion instruments. Ms. Marks had at one point told me, "Benson loves rhythm and music. He loves experimenting with sound." However, for several minutes his music had remained unusually quiet. Instead, with some effort, Benson turned his head to observe the restaurant scene. He was labeled as having Joubert syndrome, a genetically based developmental disability that results in physical disabilities. Benson was able to walk slight distances but generally used a wheelchair if he had to travel more than a few feet. His speech was extremely limited and difficult to understand. Developmental assessments suggested global delays, including cognitive disabilities.

Eventually, one of the boys who had been a restaurant patron left the dramatic play and stumbled over Benson in a silly, exaggerated fashion. The boy landed beside him. He then rolled over Benson who laughed and shrieked. Both boys giggled. On hearing the shriek, Ms. Marks cut short the roughhousing. The boy continued on, and Benson lifted himself slightly and angled himself toward the restaurant.

Ms. Marks interpreted Benson's effort as interest and called to one of her associates, Jeff Chisolm. "Hey Jeff, can you help out Benson? I think he's hungry and needs to order something."

Mr. Chisolm scooped Benson into his arms and said, "Do you want to go out to eat at the restaurant?"

Benson arched backward and opened his mouth in a wide smile, a signal for the idea of "Yes" or "This pleases me." Mr. Chisolm sat Benson in a cube chair and kneeled behind him, keeping one hand on Benson's upper back. He put a menu into Benson's hand while talking to another child. Mr. Chisolm did not realize the menu was upside down.

Benson waited for a brief second, then thrust his head backward, touching Mr. Chisolm, who looked and said, "Benson, my man, your menu is upside down! What are you doing ordering upside down?"

Benson's mouth opened wide, and he laughed. All indications suggested Benson was aware his menu was upside down, but that he did not have the coordination to easily turn it.

Mr. Chisolm turned his full attention to Benson, leaning over from behind, helping to open the menu, and asking, "What are you going to order? What're the choices?"

Mr. Chisolm manipulated Benson's hand to three photos on the menu while he said, "You want the hamburger? The fish sandwich? The soup? Maybe something else?"

Mr. Chisolm pointed to certain text saying, "See, like you can get country fried steak, BLTs, Reubens. Man, now I'm getting hungry."

Benson again laughed at Mr. Chisolm's humor. His arm, slightly supported by Mr. Chisolm, swung toward the menu, and he appeared to hit the photo of the hamburger.

"You want a burger?" Mr. Chisolm asked. "We'll order you a burger." Benson arched backward with a wide smile. Mr. Chisolm yelled, "Hey, waiter. We need you waiter."

Tristian, the waiter, marched over with the same look of exasperation he had for every customer. He looked not at Mr. Chisolm but at Benson and said, "What'll you have, Benson?"

"What are you ordering?" Mr. Chisolm said. Benson leaned forward, almost touching his head to the menu. Mr. Chisolm said, "That's right. He's getting a burger with all the fixings and double up on the fries."

Tristian scribbled on his pad saying, "You better have eight hundred dollars."

Mr. Chisolm yelped, "Eight hundred dollars, are you kidding? We're ordering a burger, man, not the whole menu."

Benson laughed and snorted, almost toppling from the chair. His body convulsed with a second laugh. Tristian went to the play kitchen and arranged a plastic hamburger and plastic fries on a plastic plate.

Another child sat down at Benson's table and asked, "May I have a bite of your hamburger, Benson?"

Benson responded by looking toward the instruments he had left behind. Both Mr. Chisolm and the child followed his glance. The child asked, "You want to drum?"

Benson arched back into Mr. Chisolm, who said, "Holy yes. That's a big yes on that!"

With Benson's friend beside him, Mr. Chisolm carried Benson back to the instruments, where the two children began making an extraordinary racket.

Local Understanding

Local understanding envisions an individual's citizenship or right to full community participation, literate and otherwise, and crafts responsive contexts within which one's active citizenship might be fostered and realized. In contrast to the still prevalent use of educational segregation to remove children with complex disability-related needs from the general early childhood community, Benson's very presence in the Sunshine Room hinted at a sense of his fundamental right to belong.

Beyond supporting his presence in the inclusive classroom, surrounding adults demonstrated local understanding through their interpretation of Benson as a child actively seeking participation and the construction of meaning. Ms. Marks, for instance, noticed Benson's body position and assumed he was signaling interest in the pretend play. She immediately alerted Mr. Chisolm, who moved Benson effectively into the play. Mr. Chisolm, as an adult, potentially could have impeded the flow of the play, but, instead, he appeared to fit within it. Throughout the interaction, he addressed Benson in a manner reflecting Benson's intelligence and full citizenship.

Whereas other children were able to independently grab menus and shout out orders with their voices, thus influencing the scenario, Benson's physical struggles required he await adult support as well as adult translation of his intent. Still, in part because of Mr. Chisolm's skills, Benson did influence the course of the play. He was able to participate in ordering and receiving his food. Benson created a space within the play that other children wanted to join.

Based on the adult models, the other children in the room also demonstrated local understanding in their assumption of Benson's full citizenship and their capacity to construct narratives that allowed for Benson's active entry and participation. The roughhousing demonstrated Benson's acceptance among his peers. When Tristian moved in to take the food order, he did not look to Mr. Chisolm but addressed Benson directly. Similarly, when the friend sat at the table at the end of the scene, she asked Benson, not Mr. Chisolm, if she might share his food. There appeared to be an organic naturalness to these interactions demonstrating the power of early childhood inclusion.

Current 1:   Making Sense of the Sign-Based Narratives of Others

Fundamental to literate citizenship is the developing understanding that others have meaningful narratives to express. Young children with significant developmental disabilities must be exposed to and actively connect with other children's symbolic presence, construction of meaning, and transformation of sign systems. This, of course, requires that children be in environments swirling with stories expressed by peers, heard on audiotapes and DVDs, run on the computer, read, collaboratively created, played and acted, told by teachers, danced, drawn, retold, remembered by visiting grandparents, and so forth.

Benson, of course, was in this type of thriving narrative vortex. *Restaurant* was one theme being emphasized the week of the observation. Over the course of the week, the children went on a field trip to a restaurant, read books about restaurants, and engaged in small group work that invoked ideas or images of restaurants. For instance, one small group, centered on one-to-one correspondence, had the children paste a certain number of paper French fries to a plate. Benson, along with all the other children, was exposed to countless restaurant narratives. Although he was developing new ways to think about and consider restaurants, he really was developing and deepening ways to organize, theorize, imagine, and make sense of the surrounding world.

In this dramatic play scenario, Benson and his peers were provided a play context initially arranged by teachers to steer the drama in the direction of restaurants. The narratives that emerged could never have been imagined by the teachers. Benson took time to first watch and perhaps to consider the ongoing stories emerging from the play prior to indicating a desire to join. With adult support, he then joined the ongoing narrative.

Often, the primary emphasis in relation to the communication and literacy of a child with significant developmental disabilities centers on the child him- or herself. The questions abound. "What is it you want?" or "What do you need?" Only later, if ever, do we have the child seriously consider the narratives of others.

In contrast, my research suggested that we might emphasize the child's active participation in the stories of others as a route to telling one's own story or generating one's own narrative. In a Vygotskian sense, to take on the role of generating narratives, a child must be in an environment where narratives are generated and the child is provided active opportunities to engage and help sustain the narratives of others. In Chapter 1, I noted that Isaac, born with trisomy 21, initially was sent to a segregated preschool for children with severe disabilities where his father described very little interaction taking place and his mother noted the absence of books, dress-up clothing and toys, music, and so forth. When in a location of narrative stagnation, there is a severe risk that a person's capacity to interact with and generate narratives will stagnate.

When participating in the narratives of others, the young child with significant developmental disabilities is in the process of generating signs. Participation is never passive. Each child, including the child with disabilities, is connecting to or making sense of the ongoing story in a highly individualized, purposeful, intellectual, and emotional manner, whether from a book, a peer, a teacher, a computer program, or some other source. The specific interpretation by that child results in the generation of new signs. So when Benson joined in the ongoing story, he helped sustain that story with adult support but did so by generating contributing signs (e.g., his signal to reorient the menu and his participation in ordering food). He also did so through his gregarious laughter, which indicated delight but also an understanding of the ongoing humor brought by Mr. Chisolm to the dramatic play.

Over the course of the academic year in the Sunshine Room, Benson accomplished the following three IEP goals related to making sense of the narratives of others:

1. Benson will indicate interest in and join in peer dramatic play with minimal adult support.

2. Benson will use his communication cards to respond to content questions about storybooks.

3. Benson will develop computer skills with the support of adults and peers.

In addition, on the developmental assessment's learning accomplishments profile, Benson made steady progress. In the personal/social domain, his scores suggested movement from well below 36 months to approximately 40–42 months. In the language/literacy domain, he also moved from untestable to approximately 38 months. Table 1 provides a series of literacy goals, general activity examples, and descriptions of how those examples may foster making sense of the narratives of others.

Current 2:   Finding and Expressing Meaning in One's Own Experience Through Narratives Crafted from Visual, Orthographic, or Tactile Sign Systems

---

Important to literacy development is the need for a child to understand that his or her own experiences, ideas, and emotions are worthy of expression and can be conveyed through visual, orthographic, or tactile sign systems. Children with significant developmental disabilities must be understood as full and valued citizens of the classroom with rich experiences, ideas, and stories to share. In the previously described restaurant scenario, Benson started out alongside the play, created a visual sign indicating his interest to join the drama, was supported within the play to become a part of the narrative, made use of the menu print and photos to add to the narrative by indicating his choice with an adult's support, interacted with peers, and then made a visual sign inviting a friend to join him back at the instruments. At each point, he was expressing dimensions of his own narratives and telling his own stories.

In addition to the signs just described, Benson also had a computer Dynavox communication device that was rarely used. His teacher said, "We do need to start using that more, but it just doesn't fit our day very often. We need to get some help," which referred to needing someone with expertise in assistive communication technology to help the classroom personnel make better use of the voice-output system. Also, Benson had a communication book made up of pages covered with computer-generated symbols with captions indicating dozens of useful words. The captioned symbols were stuck to the pages with Velcro and could be moved to a blank board so the teacher might choose only certain symbols to display.

Toward the back of the communication book were several pages of symbols drawn by Benson's peers specifically for Benson's communication and participation. "This is how Benson talks," one child told me as she showed me some of the drawings she had made for the book. Benson's teachers also made extensive use of white boards to assist Benson with his production of narratives. For instance, an adult might quickly jot out in alphabetic print two choices for Benson, touch and tell him the choices, and have him gaze or gesture toward his desired response. These white boards were also used throughout

Table 1. Literacy goals, general activity examples, and how those examples may foster making sense of the narratives of others

Literacy action	Possible general scenario	Examples of making sense of the sign-based narratives of others	Examples of finding and expressing meaning in one's own experience through narratives crafted from sign systems
Actively use the experiences and imagination of children in the classroom to develop dramatic, pretend, and imaginative play opportunities. Children with significant developmental disabilities will learn that their own experiences and stories, as well as those of their peers, can be translated into various symbolic and sign modes used in play that assist in all children's efforts to construct meaning of their surrounding world.	Seek input from children's interests to develop themes around which classroom curricula can be organized.	A student's infant sibling requires extensive hospitalization. After consulting with parents, the teacher develops a week-long theme of doctors and hospitals.	Through discussions with the parent of the child with disabilities, the teacher learns one favorite activity is grocery shopping.
	Using child-centered themes, develop props and play environments that will inspire dramatic narratives.	The teacher sets up a doctor's office and hospital in the classroom.	The teacher sets up a market area in the classroom with empty food containers, shelves, carts, and a check-out area.
	Support the active participation of children with significant developmental disabilities. Explore combinations of pictures, printed language, available assistive technology, movement, music, and so forth to promote communication within the play scenario.	The child with disabilities is supported in the role of patient. The support teacher helps the child hit a xylophone to respond to the "doctor's" questions. Other children join in the novel experience with great delight, experimenting with musical sound to express pretend ailments.	The child with disabilities is supported in all areas of play—making lists, acting as a customer, paying for groceries, restocking shelves, acting as a cashier, and so forth.
Turn text into an active experience (e.g., role play storybooks, stories generated by children). Children with significant developmental disabilities will learn that text or symbols crafted by themselves or another may express experience, both real and fantasy, and that written stories may be translated into multiple signs.	Gather storybooks relevant to curricular theme or have children express a story that is written down by the teacher.	The teacher brings in *Evan Early* (Wojahn, 2006) (a story in which an older sister describes her sibling born prematurely), *Going to the Hospital* (Rogers, 1988), *Five Little Monkeys Jumping on the Bed* (Christelow, 1989) (a story in which monkeys require medical intervention after falling off the bed), *Curious George Goes to the Hospital* (Rey & Rey, 1966), and others.	Through home and school communication, the teacher learns that the child with disabilities enjoys Maurice Sendak's Little Bear cartoons. The teacher brings in the book *Maurice Sendak's Little Bear: Father's Flying Flapjacks* (Minarik, 2002).

Read with the whole group or small group inviting active questions and commentary.	The teacher obtains a second copy of most of the books read so that the child with disabilities can hold a copy while listening and can gesture toward points of interest.	The teacher reads to the whole group. The child with disabilities assists with page turning.
Have children act out stories read.	A visiting music teacher plays guitar while the children sing, dance, and gesture to the song *Five Little Monkeys*. In particular order, children exit the central dance area as they "fall off the bed." A child with disabilities is supported by the teacher to dance and exit the area. Peer models also assist.	The class acts out the story. The child with disabilities is supported as Little Bear. The class watches an animated version of the story to compare and discuss.
Turn experience or imagination into text or another sign system (e.g., group journaling, letter writing, song writing, dance development). Children with significant developmental disabilities will learn that their own or another's thought and activity may be translated into sign and symbol that can be captured, fixed, and conveyed or interpreted. Determine a topic with the whole group, small group, or individual based on recent experience.	The teacher tells the children they are going to write a letter of thanks to the medical physician who visited the class as part of the doctor and hospital theme and brought various medical tools, pictures, and books to share with the class.	The child with disabilities brings in a disk of digital photos depicting his family's recent move to a new neighborhood. The parent included a brief list explaining each picture.

(continued)

107

Table 1. (continued)

Literacy action	Possible general scenario	Examples of making sense of the sign-based narratives of others	Examples of finding and expressing meaning in one's own experience through narratives crafted from sign systems
Actively listen to and watch books being read aloud, storytelling, puppet shows, felt board stories, and dramas. Children with significant developmental disabilities will learn that participating as a member of an audience is not a passive experience, but one that requires intellectual and emotional engagement as the story is analyzed, interpreted, and made understandable.	Turn the topic into text (or song or painting or dance) seeking each child's input.	The teacher attaches a large sheet of paper to the wall to write the thank you note. Each child expresses a favorite part of the physician's visit. The teacher writes, "Linda liked listening to a heartbeat through the stethoscope." The child with disabilities has a series of three captioned photos depicted on a laptop computer screen. He is asked to gaze toward a favorite aspect of the visit. After the selection is interpreted, the teacher asks, "Is that what you want to say?" The child indicates "Yes" through body movement.	The language therapist opens two photos on screen. She asks, "Which shows house? Which shows yard." She then captions the photos "new house" and "new yard." This is repeated with the rest of the photos. Using a laptop with voice-output technology, the teacher and the child present the photos to the class.
	In whole or small group, read a story to children while commenting on the pictures.	The teacher reads *Curious George Goes to the Hospital.*	The teacher asks the child with disabilities and a peer to help create a list of rules for the class to follow when it attends a community theater production. The teacher says, "When we attended the clarinet concert, how did we need to behave?" She then presents choices, "Loud or quiet? Move around or sit?"

| Hear complex language patterns and rhythms of literature through recitations, poetry, stories, and so forth. Children with significant developmental disabilities will develop an awareness that literature has a different, potentially more complex structure and rhythm than does spoken language. Children will develop a sense of the connection between spoken language and written language through the stories, songs, and poetry of others, but that writing is not simply "talk written down," nor is talk "written language spoken." | Actively involve all children, including the child with significant developmental disabilities, through the use of questioning. | The teacher points to the picture of character Betsy in *Curious George*. She asks, "How is Betsy feeling?" The support teacher whispers to the child with significant developmental disabilities to touch the "feelings" icon on the Dynavox screen. A new window opens with a range of feelings illustrated and captioned. The support teacher raises her hand to indicate that the student wants to respond. The student touches the icon for "scared." The voice-output expresses, "scared." The teacher asks, "Why scared?" Another child responds. | The teacher and children present a written list of determined rules to the class. The teacher asks, "Does anyone have other rules we should include?" |
| | Present complex language patterns in multiple modalities to allow children to have some control over pacing and rhythm. | The teacher inserts *Little Critter: My Trip to the Hospital* (Mayer, 1992) interactive software into the computer. The child with disabilities sits next to a typically developing child. The children place their hands on the mouse, maneuvering it together. The children click to start the story voiced by the computer and can stop the story with a click. The children click on the rhyming words link. | The child with disabilities chooses the *Morning Poem* (read after the morning song) from the poetry box that contains approximately 20 cards with poem and nursery rhyme titles, symbols of titles, and text on the reverse. The teacher recites the poem, and the teacher and children add new poems to the poetry box on a regular basis. |

(continued)

109

Table 1. *(continued)*

Literacy action	Possible general scenario	Examples of making sense of the sign-based narratives of others	Examples of finding and expressing meaning in one's own experience through narratives crafted from sign systems
Foster story development as a social process. Children with significant developmental disabilities will learn that they are valued members of the community who can initiate or contribute to a narrative using literate sign systems.	The teacher determines a topic as a story starter to which children in a small group or large group might contribute.	The teacher draws, cuts, and pastes a map that depicts several book characters at various locations. Each child is asked to point to a location or book character that he or she would like to visit and explain why. The teacher writes down the children's sentences. The child with significant developmental disabilities is supported to point. The teacher says, "You pointed to Grump-land (from the Grump book). Is that because you think I'm in a grumpy mood sometimes?" The child laughs and indicates an affirmative response through body motion. The teacher writes down, "I want to visit Grump-land because that's where my teacher lives." There is much laughter from all the children.	In small groups, the children have seven photocopied photos of themselves, each captioned with a day of week. The child with disabilities is supported by the occupational therapist. The children are told to pick a color to color themselves for Monday. The child with disabilities is given three color choices. With support, the child colors the Monday photo. Using the communication board, the child is asked, "How does *red* feel?" The child points to the captioned symbol HAPPY. The therapist writes, "Monday is red. Monday is happy."

Provide systematic opportunities to organize and express ideas related to surrounding narratives using multiple sign system modalities, including photographs, drawings, computer animation, written words in various fonts, letters combined to form words, movement and dance, props for dramatic play, and so forth. Children with significant developmental disabilities will learn that there are multiple ways to tell stories and that some materials and systems might be of more use, be more efficient, or be more reflective of intent.	Expand on children's contributions through various sign modalities.	The children draw and/or paint pictures depicting their choice of lands to visit. The child with significant developmental disabilities is supported to do an Internet image search and to scour class photos on the computer to find characters (including the teacher) to inhabit "Grump-land."	The children are encouraged to add drawings around the photo. The child with disabilities is supported to print pictures from the Internet and assisted to cut and paste. The class reads *My Many Colored Days* by Dr. Seuss (1996).
	Choose a series of nursery rhymes and children's poetry to recite and/or discuss pictures.	The teacher recites Shel Silverstein's *Unicorn Song*. The child with disabilities holds a copy and engages in the pictures.	The teacher asks the child with disabilities to choose one vehicle from several toy vehicles placed in front of her. The child gestures toward the semi-truck.
	Sing along with the children to poetry, play instruments, and listen to and sing with recordings.	The class sings *Unicorn Song*, accompanied by instruments and listens to the Irish Rover version. The child with disabilities chooses an instrument.	The teacher writes transportation on the white board. She comments on its length and sound. She asks the class, "What kind of transportation did you choose?" She writes *truck* on the white board.
	Have the children act out a story or poem.	Various roles are created for some of the children. They act out the poem while the rest of the class sings. The child with disabilities is supported in a prominent role.	The child with disabilities is helped to divide toys into four categories of transportation.
	Have the children engage interactive software to further explore poetry and its animation and/or sound.	The child with disabilities is joined by two peers at the computer. They use interactive software of Silverstein's (1974) *Where the Sidewalk Ends*.	The child with disabilities is asked to choose a favorite transportation. He indicates "train" using a picture of a train and other forms.

(continued)

Table 1. *(continued)*

Literacy action	Possible general scenario	Examples of making sense of the sign-based narratives of others	Examples of finding and expressing meaning in one's own experience through narratives crafted from sign systems
Develop awareness of and interaction with environmental print and symbols. Children with significant developmental disabilities will learn that the textual messages surrounding them in the classroom may contain important and useful narrative information.	Make use of stable, long-term print and symbols. Many teachers begin the year with text already in place on the walls and ceilings. For instance, children's names and birthdays may be displayed in a calendar-like fashion, shelves and bins may be labeled with captions and photos for replacing materials, areas of the room may be labeled, and furniture and objects may be labeled. Rather than allowing this form of print and image to fade into a background buzz, teachers actively make use of the captions and labels.	The teacher announces clean-up time: "Ray and Duanta are responsible for cleaning up this area." She holds up a card that matches a label in one area of the room. "What area is it?" The child with disabilities has access to this print and symbols as part of the communication system.	The child with disabilities contributes to stable, long-term print by matching photos of children to their names to be hung up on the birthday chart.

Make use of stable, daily environmental print and symbols. The most effective early childhood classrooms make use of daily routines that often involve print and other symbols. For instance, calendar time is a daily period when children discuss the day of the week, the schedule for the day, the current weather, and so forth. All of these topics are encoded in print and symbols and may illustrate the active importance of literacy.

Make use of novel environmental print and symbol opportunities. These opportunities present themselves on a regular basis when classroom themes change and new materials and books are brought in or when something of interest arises in the classroom that teachers and children deem worthy of documentation.

The teacher points to a line on the schedule. She asks, "What comes after lunch?" The children, recognizing the word and attached symbol, respond, "Outside time!" The teacher points to the window. She says, "During weather we talked about the snow outside. Let's make a list of what we'll need to get on when it's time to go outside." The children generate ideas, and the teacher writes them down. The child with disabilities is presented with a choice of three pictures organized before the meeting.

During a whole group circle, the teacher places an egg-shaped felt piece on the board. She sticks on the caption "egg." She says, "Something exciting started to happen last night. What might that be?" The children are quiet. She pulls on the felt egg. A precut upper half comes off as though it is cracked. A child yells, "The eggs are hatching." Several students run to the incubator. On returning to the meeting area, the teacher places a chick-shaped piece of felt on the felt board. She writes out *chick* and places it under. She asks, "How many chicks have hatched so far?" The child with disabilities is given a choice, "Did you see one, two, or three chicks?" The child responds by gesturing to three. The teacher says, "I think we counted just two so far but you're right, we're about to have three and probably even more!"

The child with disabilities is shown two jobs from the job chart. He chooses the job of host for the day. At snack and lunch, the host makes sure everyone is seated before eating and asks questions to spur conversation. The child with disabilities has a list of questions premade by the teacher and used by all children with adult support. The child with disabilities is supported to gesture to questions.

The child with disabilities is chosen as "child of the week." He brings in captioned photos from home that are discussed at their meeting and that remain on display throughout the week.

(continued)

Table 1. (continued)

Literacy action	Possible general scenario	Examples of making sense of the sign-based narratives of others	Examples of finding and expressing meaning in one's own experience through narratives crafted from sign systems
	Create and use a word wall. Commonly used words or novel words are written on cards and hung on a particular area of the wall, generally organized either alphabetically or in logical categories. For inclusive early childhood classrooms, symbols or pictures may be added to the words. Actively use the word wall. When a word comes up or a child has a question about a word, travel to the wall to look at it.	The teacher says, "Let's add words from this morning to our word wall. What words should we add?" The children decide on *chick* and *hatch*. The teacher writes out both words. She walks to the word wall and asks, "Where should *chick* go?" A child yells out, "With animals!" The teacher says, "Since it starts with a C we'll put it next to cow, our other C animal at the moment. Where should *hatch* go?" Silence. One child finally says, "With animals?" The teacher says to the child with disabilities, "Do you think *hatch* should go with animals, actions, or feelings? This is a tough one." The child gazes to animals. The teacher says, "She thinks animals, too. Certainly the chick who hatched is an animal, but to hatch is to do something." Another child yells, "Actions!" The teacher says, "I agree. I think that's best. Since *hatch* starts with an *H* we'll put it next to *hit*."	At least once per week, the class focuses on the word wall and practices signing each word. The child with disabilities relies on signed English for much of his communication.

Develop vocabulary through word and world knowledge. Children with significant developmental disabilities will expand vocabulary through exposure to and experiences with complex, descriptive language.

Discuss, write, create poetry, act out, play, dance, and read about every topic possible. If a child has a question, conduct research through books and the Internet. Share the question and the discovery with all the children.

Represent discussion and play in multiple modalities. Use sign language with key words in a discussion or dramatic play, write out important words on a white board, and create quick line drawings. Doing so alters the pace of "talk." All children will see metaphor and transduction, and children who use alternative communication will have pauses within which to join the discussion or play.

After making French toast the teacher asks, "Where does syrup come from?" With adult support, the child with disabilities and a peer explore the question using the Internet. They print out, cut, and paste an explanatory poster. They present it to the class.

The teacher has smoothie recipe steps written and symbolized on a large sheet. In large group, the children watch and participate in following the steps. A child asks, "How do you make ice?" During the discussion, the teacher writes on the white board *Freeze water.* She uses the American Sign Language sign for FROZEN WATER. The child with disabilities is supported along with peers to make the sign for ice.

The child with disabilities indicates an interest in insects. The teacher develops a theme of the week around bugs and insects, bringing in an ant farm, butterfly tent, and other items. The children explore the ground outside. Lots of new vocabulary words are discussed.

During bug and insect week, daily yoga is translated into insect positions. The child with disabilities is supported by a physical therapist.

(continued)

Table 1. *(continued)*

Literacy action	Possible general scenario	Examples of making sense of the sign-based narratives of others	Examples of finding and expressing meaning in one's own experience through narratives crafted from sign systems
Build alphabetic letter knowledge, sound–letter correspondence, and understanding of relationships across letters, graphemes, morphemes, and the phonetics of spoken language. Children with significant developmental disabilities will build on existing language skills by actively exploring parts of alphabetic print and speech.	On a long strip of paper, write a sentence relevant to the discussion.	The teacher writes a sentence strip that reads, "Jamie has a new baby sister who is beautiful!"	Using the communication board, the child with disabilities indicates a desire to write a sentence about Mom. The teacher writes, "My Mom works at Wegmans."
	Cut apart sentences into words and have children rearrange them into silly sentences.	The teacher cuts sentences into component words. The children rearrange them. The child with disabilities is given a turn.	The teacher cuts sentences into component words. The children rearrange them. The child with disabilities is given a turn.
	Cut words into graphemes and letters emphasizing letter shapes, patterns, sounds, graphemic sounds, and initial sound of morphemes.	The teacher cuts the name *Jamie* into four sections, leaving the *ie* together. She has the children put it back together. The teacher asks the child with disabilities, "Which piece comes first?"	The teacher cuts the word *Mom* into component letters. She shows how it reads the same forward and backward. She discusses capital *M*.
	Ask children to rearrange clipped-apart words into silly words.	A child rearranges the word to spell *ie-m-j-a*. The teacher tries to pronounce it.	The teacher cuts *Wegmans* into three parts: *Weg, man,* and *s*. The children experiment with rearrangement.

the day by adults who wrote out key words from ongoing activities. Sometimes this was specifically for Benson, but often all of the children participated.

Benson, Burke (described previously in this chapter), and the preschool research participants involved in Buckley's language studies did not demonstrate conventional literate citizenship. All had been measured with moderate to severe cognitive delays. Because of physical, motor, and speech difficulties, moving broadly from fantasy play to drawing to print was simply not feasible or possible. Had teachers waited for this conventional or developmental route, the children might never have been introduced to literacy-based sign systems.

Many children with significant developmental disabilities remain segregated from sign systems associated with literate citizenship because skills commonly considered to be precursors to literate readiness are not demonstrated. The result, of course, is aliteracy, subliteracy, or illiteracy. This denial of the tools of literacy need not occur. Nor do we need to think in terms of preliteracy. When a child is born, he or she has the drive to know the world symbolically, whether he or she has disabilities or not. The child is literate, and we need to foster this desire to construct narratives in every way possible.

Responsive teachers, grounded in local understanding, intuitively realize the importance of providing opportunities for the child with significant developmental disabilities to engage visual, orthographic, or tactile sign systems to construct narratives. Responsive teachers also realize that these opportunities may need to vary (even dramatically) from what is currently considered best, developmentally appropriate, or so-called evidence-based practice because the child with disabilities may exhibit developmental idiosyncrasies that preclude following the majority path.

In Chapter 2, I described a continuum of young children's sign-based expression running from the representational to the communicative. On the representational side, the sign maker is most focused on him- or herself, crafting play, pictures, dance, movement, or writing that most aptly and satisfactorily represents the current narrative. On the communicative side, the sign maker is most focused on his or her audience and its understanding of the message as he or she attempts to encode his or her feelings, emotions, thoughts, or ideas in a way that most aptly shares the narrative with others. Representation is most focused on the internal satisfaction of the sign maker, and communication is most focused on the audience of the sign maker. The continuum idea suggests that representation and communication are never exclusive of one another, but rather that the child's construction of signs emphasizes one side or the other in varying degrees at any particular moment.

For typically developing preschoolers, speech is the primary modality on the communicative end of the continuum. (Speech in the form of self-talk also extends to the representational end). On the representational end, we tend to primarily find the sign systems associated with young children's play, art, and early writing efforts. This is evident, for instance, when an adult asks the young child, "Who are you pretending to be?" or "What is this a drawing of?" The child, startled out of his or her world, must then shift from the representational side of the continuum toward the communicative side—speech—to explain his or her play or drawing to the audience.

In contrast, children with significant developmental disabilities, such as Benson, Burke, and the preschoolers in Buckley's studies, commonly experience extraordinary struggles with speech. They also commonly experience tremendous physical, motoric, and kinesthetic obstacles to engaging sign systems associated with the representational (e.g., drawing, dance, writing with crayons). Therefore, they are commonly interpreted to be entirely off the continuum from both the communicative and representational ends. On their own, they may not be speaking, signing, writing, drawing, or dramatizing in understandable, decipherable fashion.

Successful efforts to develop the literate citizenship of young children with significant developmental disabilities, always based on local understanding, recognize that indeed the child need not be off the continuum, but that he or she has a symbolic presence and is able to construct and interpret narrative, as well as learn sign systems through which narratives might be crafted or interpreted. These dimensions hinge on a deeply individualized exploration of the multitude of visual, orthographic, or tactile sign systems most commonly associated with the representational side of the expressive continuum that is wrenched or shifted toward the communicative side in a somewhat altered fashion. In short, those sign systems first explored by typically developing children as more representational than communicative (e.g., pictures, body movements, dance, the signs of play, early alphabetic writing) are explored by the child with significant developmental disabilities, in conjunction with an adult, as communicative systems.

From my research, I believe this wrench or shift of sign systems from the representational toward the communicative in early childhood is a profound alteration that is necessary for the literate citizenship of young children with significant developmental disabilities. Enacting this shift is fraught with potential dangers. If thoughtlessly done, young children's use of sign systems may end up stalled and stagnant and the child him- or herself will be blamed. Stagnation and the derivative appearance of confusion or disinterest in a sign system (generally interpreted as a manifestation of cognitive delay) arises because professionals may neglect the child's transformational authority that is so fundamental to typically developing children's development of visual, orthographic, or tactile sign systems.

As described in Chapter 4, children never merely recreate a sign but are always in the process of creating new signs. We must not forget this in our literate approach to children with significant developmental disabilities. When we turn traditional representational sign systems into communicative ones, we must not strip the representational qualities from those systems. For instance, the symbols arranged on a laminated board in order for a child with significant developmental disabilities to point for communicative purposes are often miniature, highly abstract line drawings downloaded from a computer program. Typically developing children make their own drawings and early letterings, but children with significant developmental disabilities are commonly exposed primarily to premade images that are imposed on them. This has a way of obscuring and pacifying the child's potential transformational involvement in the use of those images for communication.

In contrast, the child's use of premade symbols (whether laminated or appearing on screen as icons) should be treated as the construction of new signs just as the interpretation of a storybook is the child's construction of a new sign (see Chapter 4). For example, when the child who uses a communication aid gestures or gazes toward the symbol for bathroom (generally a line drawing of a toilet), that nanosecond of communication may appear very similar to another child's gesture to a similar symbol or another child saying out loud, "I need to go to the bathroom." Except when we are potty training the child, we view such expressions as fairly mundane communication; however, the child is always expressing a unique narrative.

In this example, no two children ever share the same bathroom history, and in that gesture toward the symbol on the communication board is the accumulated experience of that particular child. He or she alone knows the full narrative contained in the gesture toward the sign for bathroom. We must approach the now-communicative sign construction of children with significant developmental disabilities as though it was both fully communicative and fully representational. We must not see in their gestures the mundane, but rather celebrate the same transformational creativity we see in the construction of representational signs crafted by typically developing children.

Recognizing and celebrating the expression of even simple narratives on the part of children with significant disabilities will enhance the sense of children's active, intentional, intellectual, and emotional involvement in the community. For instance, if a symbol-based communication book makes sense for the child, as it did for Benson, perhaps the child might help construct or choose the signs used. Instead of an abstract line drawing of a toilet to represent bathroom, the child might want to choose from several photos or drawings of a bathroom. Or perhaps the child would want multiple bathroom signs to reflect varying bathroom needs. Every trip to the bathroom is somewhat different, and the child might want different pictures to convey these variations, just as typically developing children use inflection and intonation to convey various and changing bathroom wants, needs, and emergencies through their voices.

In Benson's situation, his peers actually added to the symbols used. Over the course of the school year, Benson accomplished the following goals related to expressing his own narratives. First, Benson will use his communication book and/or Dynavox to complete a story during "Thinking In Stories Time" every Monday. (The teacher transcribed and embellished from the symbols Benson indicated and then asked, "Is that what you meant? Yes or No?") Second, Benson will pick a favorite book to share with the class and will respond to questions about the book using symbols and/or a Dynavox and a word board. (Table 1 provides more examples of children finding and expressing meaning in their own experience through narratives crafted from visual, orthographic, or tactile sign systems.)

Current 3:   Developing Complexity with Visual, Orthographic, or Tactile Sign Systems in Sustaining or Generating Narratives

Efforts to foster the literate citizenship of young children with significant developmental disabilities must proceed beyond rudimentary stages. Too often children become sporadically able to indicate an understandable sign for *yes, no, bathroom,* and other basic language needs, and, because consistency remains elusive, adults determine the child cannot proceed further, and efforts stall. Over the course of my literacy studies, I have heard from dozens of parents who reported that their children stopped receiving speech-language therapy services because they were not advancing at what was determined by professionals to be the required pace. Inevitably this occurred in segregated educational sites.

Had Benson initially been held to some imposed standard of advancement, he, too, would have been in danger of being eliminated from language support services. Benson was Ms. Marks's student for 2 years. When he first joined the Sunshine Room at the age of 3, he demonstrated little mobility or understandable communication. He could not hold up his head. On developmental assessments, he was basically untestable, which among professionals often translates into perceptions of severe cognitive impairments. Ms. Marks recalled,

66 Well, I was told Benson was coming to my room, and I knew he had pretty severe disabilities. I did a little reading on Joubert syndrome, so I had that, but really, I first visited him at home, and I remember scooping him up, and I looked in those eyes and I said to [Benson's] Mom, 'I think he's going to do just fine.' And I remember she just started crying, and I'm like, 'Really, this little guy has spirit.' And even then I think he smiled, but not like now—how he smiles and laughs. He's got the most developed sense of humor I've ever seen in any kid, disabled or not. Like we [adults] need to be careful how we joke. You know? He gets it all. 99

Despite Ms. Marks's local recognition that Benson belonged as a full citizen, determining how he could be an active participant of the Sunshine Room, let alone an active participant of the literate community of the Sunshine Room, was daunting. Initially, the teachers relied on extraordinarily subjective indicators of communication. Ms. Marks noted, "He's got the most beautiful eyes, and if we saw those eyes shine we figured, 'Yes.' If the eyes went dark we'd figure, 'Nope.'" From there they learned that physically positioning Benson had tremendous implications for his capacity to gesture and turn his head. This was the next stage of symbolic participation. The teachers then introduced certain symbols and object choices (e.g., two toys) toward which Benson might gaze or gesture.

At first, the teachers had great difficulty discerning Benson's intentional movement from his inadvertent movement, but the team of teachers never stopped pushing forward. The team collegiality and professionalism sustained these often frustrating efforts with not just Benson, but numerous other complex children, with disabilities and without. The teachers recognized Benson as having a symbolic presence, the capacity to construct narratives, and the ability to transform sign systems into his own. "We knew he could grow if we could grow," explained Ms. Marks. The teachers considered it their awesome and humbling charge to disavow crude, mass excuses, such as the label *intellectual disability,* and instead recognize and foster Benson's individual literate presence.

Developing and scaffolding Benson's literate presence proceeded in both directions along the early childhood expressive continuum from representational to communicative expression. Initially, the teachers were most interested in promoting forms of recognizable communication. This period did not exclude interest in the representational. Such exclusion is impossible in the inclusive early childhood classroom. To the extent teachers felt themselves capable, Benson was a part of dramatic and fantasy play, dance, poetry, storybook reading, and art projects. All of these representational efforts, of course, are not exclusive to communication; one side of the continuum is generally emphasized over the other, but elements from both edges are always drawn in.

At this point, however, the majority of focused adult energy was on ascertaining Benson's capacity to construct signs (meaning and form) given materials presented by adults, which were generally in the form of computer-generated, captioned symbols designed to represent in a simple line drawing common language (primarily nouns and verbs with a few adjectives and prepositions) considered by adults to be useful to Benson. As such, the adults presenting the symbols had their own signs (meaning and form) in mind when using Velcro to present the symbols on a black communication board to Benson. However, if Benson was to grow in sophistication, he would need to take the forms crafted by the adult world and energetically, emotionally, and intellectually ascribe his own meaning to them.

For communication to actually take place, the meaning Benson ascribed to the form (symbol with word caption) handed over by the adult should be aligned with the general understanding of others but will never absolutely mimic or mirror another's intention. As with any child, Benson will always bring his own life world along to any sign. For instance, during one activity that occurred after Benson was clearly expressing his own ideas through symbol, he was asked to list and name his family. While other children created drawings, the aide working with Benson asked him how many sisters and brothers he had. He correctly responded using gesture with some support to a written number line, and the aide placed the correct number of symbols alongside the symbols for Mom and Dad, two sisters, and two brothers, one representing himself. (The use of photographs would have been better, but the activity proceeded for Benson with abstract line drawings in which the two symbols for sister looked exactly alike and the two symbols for brother looked exactly alike, and not one symbol looked anything like Benson's actual family.)

The aide placed the four children's written names at each corner of the communication board and asked him to name the siblings. She pointed to the first sister symbol, and Benson gazed toward his eldest sister's name. She pointed to the next sister, and he gazed toward his other sister's name. She pointed to one of the brother symbols, and he leaned down gazing toward his older brother's name. When asked who the last symbol was, Benson smiled at his own name.

The adults who created or presented these symbols had particular intentions in mind, and certainly Benson, at this point in his development, conformed to those intentions, but clearly from his own life world. He purposefully made the abstract symbols into his own family. Similarly, during this activity many of his typically developing peers created drawings that looked similar; that is, large circles for heads resting on lengthy sticks for legs. However, although the signs crafted appeared to be extremely similar, no two children had the same meaning for their crafted drawings. They all brought their own particular energies and histories to the activity.

Of interest, the aide working with Benson, without knowing the answer, asked him, "Do you have a pet?" Benson arched his body indicating the affirmative. She placed the symbol for dog, cat, fish, and cow (the last causing them both to laugh) on the board and said, "Is one of these your pet?" Benson both arched forward and leaned in, bringing his arm awkwardly toward the symbol for dog.

Both the lead teacher and I had been watching with interest. The symbol for dog depicted a floppy eared, Beagle-type line image. Benson indeed had a dog, but it was a Chihuahua and looked nothing like the symbol. He had made the intellectual leap from the abstract image to his own life world!

"What's his name?" asked the aide, looking from Benson to Ms. Marks.

Ms. Marks said, "Benson, try to spell her name."

She brought an alphabet board over and held Benson's arm at the elbow to support his gesture. He flopped his arm toward what looked like either the *S* or *T*.

Ms. Marks said, "Did you want *S* or *T*?" Benson slumped as if exhausted. Ms. Marks laughed and said, "Okay, that's been a lot of work. You need a break. Tiger. The dog's name is Tiger."

As Benson's communicative abilities developed, teachers were more confident in their efforts to promote his representational expression. His active involvement in the restaurant play was an example. Ms. Marks recalled their thoughts from the previous school year:

"We knew supporting him in play and the painting and stuff was important, but it was, like, hard to say why exactly. We weren't just going through the motions, but a lot of people probably would have thought—or maybe did [think that] we were just doing it to do it…. But as you saw his meaning, his language emerge, we're like, 'A-ha, you bastards! We were right and you were wrong. Nana-nana-boo-boo.' Except maybe [we were] more mature?"

Ms. Marks was referring to the skepticism directed toward her by those who felt her intuitive belief in children's competence, that which emerged from local understanding, was too Pollyannaish.

Although certainly having communicative consequences, Ms. Marks and her teaching team also opened opportunities for Benson falling on the more traditional representational side of the continuum. For instance, I observed Benson in a standing frame, a platform device that held him vertically. On the attachable tray, a physical therapist squirted a large amount of foam shaving cream. Two peers stood along-side. The therapist asked Benson, "What color should we start with?" in reference to the color dye that should be added to the shaving cream. On a white board she had quickly scrawled a green *G*, a red *R*, and a blue *B*. Benson touched the *B*. She said, "Ah, your favorite," and she placed some drops of washable blue dye in the shaving cream. Benson and his peers proceeded to mush their hands through the cream, creating designs and play scenarios. Other peers quickly jostled to join.

The classroom computer certainly held communicative potential for Benson, but his teacher also viewed his efforts as artistic and representational. For instance, she made extensive use of the Bailey's Book House software by Edmark, which allowed Benson access to interesting alphabetic opportunities using either a single switch or an adapted keyboard. Using the software program, Benson was able to rhyme words and create poems, explore letter shapes, write songs, and simply explore typing. For instance, I observed Benson and Ms. Marks together at the computer with Ms. Marks requesting, "Benson, type your name."

Using the adaptive keyboard, Benson touched the letter *B*. Ms. Marks's hand supported his elbow. Next, he touched the letter *N*. Ms. Marks did not correct him; rather, she said, "Good job. Keep going." Next, he touched the *S*. Then, he stopped.

Ms. Marks said, "Awesome! You are awesome. Let's change fonts. Let's pick a shape you like!"

She began to change the font of Benson's typing, telling him the name of each style as she clicked. After a while, they determined the font he desired and printed out his name. Ms. Marks treated the print-out as an artistic product. She showed it to the class, which caused a degree of awe among the children, many of whom were not yet able to pick out letters on the keyboard. Benson beamed.

In the arena of significant developmental disability, the rule on the part of professionals interested in literacy has generally been to stall at the rudimentary. Such an attitude belies cultural stereotypes, not empirical evidence. We have more than a century of evidence suggesting that those who have been culturally cast as hopelessly aliterate or subliterate due to disability might in fact develop sophisticated literate citizenship when provided thoughtful opportunities. The lack of literacy lies not in the individual but in the attitudes and practices of those who surround the person with a disability. This is not to suggest that every young child with a significant developmental disability has the potential to ultimately become an acclaimed novelist, poet, composer, journalist, or artist. Rather, it means that all young children, with disabilities or without, can continuously grow in their literate profiles as long as thoughtful, responsive opportunities are presented in a context of local understanding.

Christopher Nolan, born with severe physical disabilities, described years of community separation and the presumption of incompetence until his parents introduced him at age 11 to a computer. In the preface to Nolan's autobiography, John Carey described what happened next.

> He plummeted into language like an avalanche, as if it were his one escape route from death—which, of course, it was. He had been locked for years in the coffin of his body, unable to utter. When he found words he played rapturously with them, making them riot and lark about, echoing, alliterating and falling over one another. (2000)

Nolan was not intrinsically separated from the surrounding world. He had a symbolic presence and the capacity to craft narratives through which meaning was made, as well as the ability to transform sign systems into his own. What was required was a local sense of his capacity and the correct tools, opportunities, and perseverance to unleash his potential.

Current 4: Deriving Joy and Other Affective Forces from Critical, Reflective Engagement with Visual, Orthographic, and Tactile Sign Systems

---

Developing sophistication with sign systems for children with significant developmental disabilities is most effective when children experience the tremendous intellectual and emotional thrill that occurs while discovering the ideas and stories of others and in sharing and connecting their own stories. For children without disabilities, the emotions and cognitive energy associated with getting lost in a story (or art or play) are recognized and valued in terms of promoting general development. This must be a part of *all* children's experiences.

In the restaurant play scenario, Benson greatly enjoyed engaging both with the teacher's aide and his peers. Benson's clear delight appeared to attract peer interaction that provided a meaningful and natural context to support his developing capacity with various sign systems. In a similar fashion, Isaac (see Chapter 1) displayed the sheer exuberance of getting lost in his favorite storybook and ultimately teaching the class how to dance to text! Furthermore, as described in Chapter 3, a best friendship between Lori, with significant developmental disabilities, and Starr, without disabilities, blossomed in the library section of the classroom and provided both Lori and Starr with numerous opportunities to further their use of literate sign systems. In every case, the energies associated with fun, joy, and motivation were at the heart of the children's pursuits, use, and expansion of sign systems.

In an era of educational high stakes testing where formalized drill in a rigid version of literacy has now burst into kindergarten and even preschool, the realization of the importance of joy and other affective forces to all young children's learning is dissolving. This is an extraordinarily destructive trend. Children's literacy begins with their symbolic presence—the primordial drive to form a coherent understanding of the surrounding world. Children construct meaning through narratives crafted from a vast array of sign systems. These early efforts hinge on motivation and drive that erupts forth from children when they are a part of thoughtful, engaging contexts. The inclusive early childhood classroom inherently involves information, ideas, and communication contained in a variety of visual, orthographic, and tactile sign systems. Children participating therein are self-actuated to transform these systems into their own to make ever deeper and more sophisticated sense of the surrounding world.

Learning and development in the early years is integrally linked to children's motivation. When there exists a meaningful reason to make use of particular symbols and sign systems, children will do so in a driven, highly intentional manner. No research evidence exists to prove that adult imposition of drill and rote memorization exercises in preschool and kindergarten has anywhere near the power of a child's own drive, certainly fostered by adults and a thoughtful context, to know, take on, make sense of, deepen, and transform the sign systems of communication and representation.

There is a universal agreement among child developmentalists that children are driven to make sense of their surrounding world, that it is a social drive involving interaction and collaboration with others, and that this forms the basis of literacy. A common caveat among these scientists of childhood, however, has been the qualifier that children's constructivism is ascribed only to those who are "normal," "healthy," or some other euphemism for not having disabilities. Howard Gardner (1991), for instance, when describing the preschool years as the *age of symbols*, explained that he was talking only about "*normal* children the world over" (p. 56).

Eliminating from young children with disabilities a basic sociointellectual drive is fundamentally dehumanizing. The pseudologic that motivation must be imposed through the use of reinforcers, punishments, and aversives derived from the psychological school of thought known as behaviorism then becomes the issue. Indeed, segregated special education classrooms arranged around the idea of moderate to severe disability have become the final bastion of efforts to mimic learning theory laboratories where rats and pigeons were trained through operant conditioning techniques, a subcategory of behavior modification. These sterile early childhood locations in no way approximate the lively, noisy, interactive hubbub of the inclusive early childhood educational community. Indeed, Edgar (1997) described special education as a fundamentally broken system and expressed what he referred to as *disappointment* that "children with disabilities were not finding more joy in their lives" (p. 323).

Although no preschool or kindergarten day is without moments of teasing, anger, tears, or distress, the children involved in my studies and exemplified throughout this book in various ethnographic scenarios, generally experienced the kind of joy and motivation we should expect in early childhood education. The key ingredients appear to be an inclusive environment and local understanding. Inclusion opens for all children the opportunities inherent in a vital, engaging, responsive early childhood education context. Local understanding assures that thoughtful and intense effort will be exerted so that every child can actively develop a connectedness that fosters full citizenship.

THE BASIC SKILLS–PHONICS MODEL AND YOUNG CHILDREN WITH SIGNIFICANT DEVELOPMENTAL DISABILITIES

As described in Chapter 2, *basic skills–phonics* is a broad term encompassing the use of adult-led direct instruction, drill, and formal exercises to first raise in children a phonemic awareness of spoken language and to next translate this awareness into sound–letter correspondence skills. Phonics has successfully dominated political and education policy debates as a panacea for America's perceived public school woes since at least the early 1990s.

As previously indicated, there is the possible importance of adults raising the awareness of a connection between spoken language and other sign and symbol systems including, of course, alphabetic writing in children with significant developmental disabilities. However, the four currents of literacy, the examples from Table 1, and the general message of this entire book emphasize efforts quite distinct from basic skills–phonics. In part, this involves the restrictive frame phonics advocates hold for what constitutes meaningful engagement with language versus my own broadened sense of literacy. However, even remaining strictly within orthographic sign systems, phonics does not appear to hold the key to the literate citizenship of young children who have serious struggles with spoken communication. Even the strictest and most virulent advocates of phonics admit this, albeit often crudely and in a manner that suggests literacy is therefore an impossibility. For instance, in her treatise that harshly dismantles all literacy efforts other than phonics, McGuinness (1997) presented what she termed to be evidence showing "any child or adult who isn't mentally retarded or deaf can be taught to read if given proper instruction" (p. 12). Throughout the remainder of the book there is no more mention of the deaf child or the child presumed to have intellectual disabilities. They are no longer important to the topic. But we can no longer afford to casually or crudely dismiss the great capacities of all children, including those with the most complex disabilities.

A commonality across the multitude of phonics programs in early childhood is that they are designed to require speech. Seemingly one may stray from design to use, for instance, internal or silent speech to accomplish the objectives of the program, but this does not appear to be the general approach of young children with significant developmental disabilities, all of whom struggle in one fashion or another with useful spoken language. Rather, Benson and the other children involved in my research, Burke, the children involved in Buckley's studies, and others appear to initially approach written words as though they are ideographs (e.g., the golden arches of McDonalds) or a picture language. The form of the word is not sounded out, but its primary or prominent features are remembered and in turn visually expressed (often on an adapted keyboard) by the child (e.g., the two Zs in the word *pizza*, the first letter of the child's name). This has less to do with sound and much more to do with the child's sense of form.

Initially approaching written language as if it were a picture system, albeit one that does not even attempt at realism, should not be shocking. As described in Chapter 4, this is precisely how preschool and kindergarten children on their own initially approach writing. Prominent features of the form of written language are recalled in an almost artistic, certainly creative effort. Ashton-Warner's (1963) Maori children did not sound out their initial written sentences and whole paragraphs. Rather, they crafted words from their key vocabularies and made logical inferences on designing more novel words needed to complete written stories. Certainly some level of sound–letter understanding was invoked, but it was not the central effort.

Similarly, Buckley's (2006) large number of preschool research participants, all described as having moderate to severe disabilities, developed vast sight word vocabularies involving hundreds of written words. This may seem incredible just given the general consensus on what is deemed possible for even typically developing 2- to 5-year-olds, but when the idea of disability is added, the reading skills appear wholly implausible. However, her participants were learning written language as a first language. Consider the vast spoken vocabularies of typically developing preschoolers and the idea of a relatively large written vocabulary for children whose speech is highly limited may not seem so amazing or even fraudulent. Indeed, some have pondered whether the stability and relative permanence of written language might actually lend itself in quite natural ways to the various neurologies of children with significant developmental disabilities.

As children with disabilities develop in sophistication, they can begin to learn internal logics involved in crafting, altering, and recrafting written language. Table 1 provides examples of visually breaking written phrases into component parts. Perhaps rather than phonics as a basic approach to orthographic literacy, we might instead refer to *graphemics* for the child with significant developmental disabilities. For more than 2 decades, Buckley (1985) has asserted that "mastering a written language is in some way easier than mastering a spoken language.... Words that are seen in their written form are retained more readily than words heard in spoken form" (p. 322).

Furthermore, although agreeing that phonics may play a useful role in some reading instruction, Buckley (1985) pointed out that "it is not essential for learning to read" (p. 327). Cossu and colleagues reported similar findings from their experimental investigations of the reading development of children with trisomy 21 who had been identified as having moderate to severe cognitive impairments (Cossu & Marshall, 1990; Cossu, Rossini, & Marshall, 1993; Cossu, Shankweiler, Liberman, Fowler, & Fisher, 1988). Their research came out at a time when many others were beginning to make absolute causal links between phonemic awareness and the ability to read. In response, Cossu and colleagues stated,

> We simply wish it to be accepted that not all children depend on phonological awareness in order to learn to read. If it is agreed that different children learn to read in different ways and that phonological awareness may play little or no role with some children, then we have no quarrel with assigning some importance to phonological awareness in the reading development of other children. (1993, p. 135)

In fact, there is a decades-old and constantly growing body of research that suggests learning to read may actually teach phonetic capacities to some children with significant developmental disabilities (Buckley, 1985, 1995, 2006; Duffen, 1979; Morais, Carey, Alegria, & Bertelson, 1979; Saunders & Collins, 1972). As a teenager, Burke, for instance, after a lengthy period of hearing his communicative typing read out loud via voice-output technology, began to read his own typing out loud (Broderick & Kasa-Hendrickson, 2001). This has slowly turned into a limited capacity to hold spontaneous conversations with his voice. The graphemes have become phonemes rather than the reverse.

Chapter 6

"His Only Limitations Were How I Imagined He Could Do Things"

Concluding Thoughts on the Literate Citizenship of Young Children with Significant Developmental Disabilities

M rs. Johansson, Isaac's mother who was introduced in Chapter 1, sat on a small couch in her son's Corner Nook classroom at the Shoshone School. Children zipped around the room in frenetic, high-octane bursts of energy and vitality. I sat beside her on a preschooler's chair, knees framing my chin. The school year was nearing its end. Isaac would return to the Corner Nook for an inclusive summer program, but in the fall he would begin general kindergarten in a nearby suburban school district.

"Look at how far we've come," Mrs. Johansson said.

We both watched Isaac, who was on all fours with several other children in the classroom loft. Their play had morphed from a home scenario where one child had been the pet dog into all the children becoming a pack of wild dogs, apparently trying to find their way through a mountain snowstorm with very little food. Isaac pulled up on his knees and howled as if the moon had crashed right through the classroom ceiling. Mrs. Johansson laughed.

The noise caught Ms. Robbins's attention. "Oh my," she called out. "The wolves are astir today."

"We ain't wolves," a child shouted.

"You *aren't?*" Ms. Robbins asked, emphasizing the correct grammar.

"Dogs is wolves," another child intoned with authority.

"Nah-ah," responded the first child, "Cats is lions."

A third child stood and ferociously roared with claws reaching out. She said, "I'm a lion! I eat dogs."

Isaac stood next to her, roared, and made his own claws. Suddenly the play morphed yet again as every child became part of a pride of lions.

Ms. Robbins, who rarely took time to converse at length with adults other than her team while the students were in the room, strode over.

Isaac's mother looked up, smiling. "I was just telling Chris, you know, how far we've come!" Ms. Robbins smiled, and I nodded. Earlier I had been looking over Isaac's most recent assessment information plus an updated IEP assessment.

I said, "You guys made a dramatic play objective for Isaac in the beginning."

Ms. Robbins laughed. "Can you believe it?" She added, "He's like the king of drama in here. I think we'll call that one accomplished."

"And," I continued, "you wanted him to recognize *five* high-frequency words by the end of the year."

Ms. Robbins again laughed. "He knows about 100 sight words," she said.

Mrs. Johansson shook her head. "I'll admit now," she said, "I thought you all were insane on that one. I wanted Isaac to be exposed to stories and everything, but I never thought he'd be a reader. I mean not like this. Not now. It wasn't even that important to me—yet. I just wanted him to be a part...." She shook her head again as her voice trailed off. "It's more than that, you know?" she said.

Ms. Robbins nodded her head. She pointed to the loft where Isaac now stood as ringmaster with an actual oversized top hat on his head and a piece of rope in his hand while the other children circled him in the roles of various exotic animals.

"It's that," said Ms. Robbins. Then, she abruptly spun around. "All right," she said, "time to get back to work," and away she strode.

Later in the day, after the students had left, Ms. Robbins and I returned to our conversation. She recounted from previous years several students who had profoundly affected her capacity to presume competence where so many other professionals might only see inability. Talk turned to Elijah, a child considered to have profound disabilities whom she had taught the previous year.

Ms. Robbins took a sip of coffee and said,

> " You know, after all these years, I really, really see it as about my imagination for a kid. Like Elijah, his only limitations were how I imagined he could do things. "

When Elijah had entered Ms. Robbins's classroom, his speech had been extremely limited and highly irregular for a 3-year-old nearing 4. His only consistently understandable word had been *no!* In addition to his communication disabilities, Elijah was also labeled as having an intellectual disability. Developmental assessments suggested he was functioning cognitively at a 9- to 11-month age range. Yet, Ms. Robbins decided that Elijah's possibilities were as expansive as her own imagination allowed. This was a radical reconfiguration of conventions that place limitations and impairments squarely within the body and brain of the person labeled, and definitely not, as Ms. Robbins had done, in the minds of those surrounding the person.

Ms. Robbins's inversion has powerful implications beyond her classroom. No longer can professionals shrug off a child's lack of citizenship, literate or otherwise, as a manifestation of organic inability. Rather, that notion is now embedded in the culture surrounding the child! Teaching has become an awesome and humbling charge.

In fact, this is precisely how New Zealand school teacher Sylvia Ashton-Warner (1963) approached her teaching. At a time when the majority of New Zealand educators wrote off in racist fashion the indigenous Maori population as educationally (meaning intellectually) inferior to the majority white population, Ashton-Warner challenged this seemingly omnipotent reality. She rejected the notion that the Maori's school-based struggles reflected rampant innate inability. Instead, she altered her own teaching to take the children's strengths, individual histories, imaginations, and motivations into account. In response, her young students experienced a deep and dramatic connectedness with the surrounding literate community.

INCLUSIVE EDUCATION AND LOCAL UNDERSTANDING: THE TRUE BASICS OF LITERATE CITIZENSHIP

Inclusive education appears to be fundamental to the literate citizenship of children with significant disabilities. In its rejection of segregated schooling, inclusion immerses students in the wonderfully chaotic play patterns, explosive language systems, and complex narrative forms of the early childhood literate community. Segregation as an approach to education is based on the idea that we must first separate children from the everyday convolution and messiness of citizenship in order to directly teach through reward and punishment how to be a citizen. In this logic, only after the child achieves the magical scores of success (developmental, communicative, social, behavioral, literate, and otherwise) that prove his or her competence apart from the valued community is the child allowed into the valued community. This logic is, of course, fundamentally flawed. A small child cannot prove his or her way into value. The child either is valued or not. A child cannot find membership apart from membership. A child cannot claim a culture if he or she is segregated from that culture. We cannot teach connectedness in the absence of connectedness.

Adults, no matter how well schooled in early childhood special education, can contrive contexts but never recreate that which is produced when a diverse range of young children come together as a singular classroom community. The result of segregation is most commonly a stagnant environment. The child's symbolic presence— the drive to imaginatively make sense and construct symbolic meaning of the surrounding world in collaboration with others—is often shattered by segregation. Thus, literate citizenship does in fact become an improbability, as does any form of valued communal participation.

Presence in a general or natural early childhood education environment is not enough. Literate citizenship on the part of young children with significant developmental disabilities hinges on active involvement with peers and thoughtful adults within that setting. Local understanding is vital in that those who share in its dynamics envision a specific young child's citizenship or right to full community participation, literate and otherwise, and proceed to draft and craft responsive contexts within which that specific child's active citizenship is fostered and realized. As the child's participatory capacities increase in sophistication, so, too, does the sense of his or her citizenship.

When Isaac first entered the Corner Nook classroom at Shoshone School, his teacher could easily have maintained any curricular plans she already had in place. Instead, she recognized the importance of developing Isaac's connectedness to the community and so adjusted her plans to highlight *Where the Wild Things Are* and some of Isaac's other favorite literature by Maurice Sendak. She knew that in this way Isaac might find an initial foothold of stability on which to expand his citizenship. She also knew that every other child would benefit from her efforts.

THE ENRICHED COMMUNITY:
INCLUSION AND LITERACY

Two concerns are commonly voiced among professionals who express resistance to inclusion. The first is that the needs of children with disabilities will not be met amid the complex dynamics of a general education setting. The second is that the needs of children with disabilities will require an excessive amount of directed resources that take away from the educational experiences of children without disabilities. From the vignettes provided throughout this book, neither concern is valid in a thoughtfully structured, well-resourced early childhood classroom.

In fact, the early childhood literate community appears to be an enriched and enlivened context for all children due to the participation of young students with significant developmental disabilities. In the inclusive early childhood literate community, the forms, functions, and content of literacy are all positively affected and broadened.

In terms of form, or modality, the traditional visual, orthographic, and tactile sign systems associated with rich, constructivist environments are maintained. Children experience text, pictures, body language, and much more through storybooks, musical composition, drawing, dance, nursery rhymes, clay, singing, dramatic play, computer programs, calendars, name tags, pâpier mâché, chants, poetry, painting, and so forth. The list is endless. In the inclusive environment, however, we also see the addition of assistive technologies with voice-output capabilities, communication boards, ASL and signed English, adapted keyboards, Braille, head sticks used as pointers for typing, increased pictorial and lettered representations of key concepts, altered pacing, standing frames, and so forth.

Clearly the early childhood education of typically developing students can proceed without these necessary adaptations for children with significant disabilities; however, experiencing these additional literate forms allows children to deeply understand the organic and democratic reality that human development occurs over a vast spectrum, not along a narrow path. This reality also places a value on the larger community and demonstrates that particular human differences may pose dilemmas to a child's connectedness, but these dilemmas are never insurmountable. Ultimately, a democratic community requires the imaginative energy and participatory effort of each member directed toward valuing and fostering the participation of all other members. We cannot truly learn democracy apart from participating in a democracy.

In the inclusive early childhood literate community, the functions of literacy traditional to constructivist classrooms are maintained.

These largely have to do with the child's representational drive to make sense of the surrounding world. Out of the synthesis of various visual, orthographic, and tactile sign systems, young children construct and engage narratives that assist in developing a coherent understanding of the contexts through which they move.

In addition, when we meet the needs of young children with significant developmental disabilities, every child in the classroom experiences the expansion of sign systems from the representational edge of the expressive continuum toward the communicative end. Symbols, systematic movement patterns (e.g., ASL), and print suddenly become vital tools for public interpersonal engagement. Children without disabilities learn that there are ways other than speech to express complex narratives. These alternative modes are clearly valued by teachers, so children come to value these approaches as well.

Finally, the great diversity experienced in inclusive environments tends to powerfully filter into the curriculum. Simply supporting the presence of children who would otherwise be segregated brings their interests, imaginations, and histories into the classroom. Isaac's love of the work of author Maurice Sendak, for instance, inspired a week's worth of literature-based activities.

Furthermore, inclusion creates a very real context for young children's critical engagement with issues related to the wonderful diversity of humanity. How are we alike? How are we different? During one circle time, Ms. Robbins read her 4- and 5-year-old students a book on smoke signals and other sign systems once used by various American Indian nations. Ms. Robbins then had her students actively generate and demonstrate a list of the many ways they had for capturing, fixing, interpreting, or conveying meaning to one another.

Ms. Robbins described one point of the activity:

> I wanted the kids to become part of our problem solving process for understanding each other. As adults in here we spend a lot of time thinking about this, but so should the kids.

In an inclusive classroom, the urgency and importance of considering multiple sign and symbol systems might be heightened for both adults and children.

LITERACY AS A CIVIL RIGHT

Denial of literate opportunities forces the abrogation of a child's civil rights and leads to lifelong subjugation. In her critical analysis of the 1954 *Brown v. Board of Education* school desegregation case, Prendergast (2002) stated, "Until the middle of the twentieth century, the dominant

U.S. educational policy was to use whatever means possible, including the force of law, to restrict access to literacy for African Americans and to preserve it for Whites" (p. 206). In the 1950s, it was estimated that more than one in four African Americans could not read or write (Kluger, 1975). The NAACP strategy in *Brown v. Board of Education* that focused on integrating public schools was in part a recognition of the cultural links between literacy and democratic citizenship.

When the five lower court cases subsumed as the case came before the U.S. Supreme Court, the lawyer defending South Carolina's segregated school system, John W. Davis, stated in his opening argument:

> May it please the Court, I think if the appellants' construction of the Fourteenth Amendment should prevail here, there is no doubt in my mind that it would catch the Indian within its grasp just as much as the Negro. If it should prevail, I am unable to see why a state would have any further right to segregate its pupils on the ground of sex or on the ground of age or on the ground of mental capacity. (As quoted in Friedman, 1969, p. 51)

Davis's hyperbole before the Supreme Court was the losing side's fearful recognition that indeed *Brown v. Board of Education* had potentially far-reaching consequences—The end to segregation of one disenfranchised category of children might well result in the equal protection of all of America's children, including African Americans, Native Americans, females, and children with presumed intellectual and other significant developmental disabilities. Therefore, historically devalued students potentially would be guaranteed equal opportunity to access crucial cultural tools for community and societal participation including, most prominently, literacy.

In an ironic twist, 17 years after Davis's statement before the Supreme Court, his words were in fact used to end the segregation of children with disabilities from public schooling. Attorney Thomas Gilhool, acting as counsel to the plaintiffs, included the Davis quote in the initial memorandum filed in the 1971 *Pennsylvania Association for Retarded Children v. Commonwealth of Pennsylvania* (Lippman & Goldberg, 1973). This was the original *equality of access to education* court case for students labeled with intellectual disabilities and would influence Congress in 1975 to pass the civil rights legislation that steadily evolved into today's Individuals with Disabilities Education Improvement Act of 2004 (PL 108-446), mandating that all children, including those with disabilities, receive an appropriate education at public expense. In 1986, the original law that focused on school-age students would be amended to include consideration of the educational needs of children from birth to kindergarten.

Translating the hazy, federal notion of *appropriate education* into its required complexity of local forms in early childhood, however, has proved difficult not only for young children with disabilities but for all children at the margins whose education is most reliant on, and most vulnerable to, broad policy and mandates. This, of course, reflects a general lack of capacity to engage educational complexity on the part of policy makers who often substitute ideological frames that have little to do with actual children and how they each learn. Thus, a bill such as No Child Left Behind, focused as it is on "low-achieving students in our Nation's highest-poverty schools, limited English proficient children, migratory children, *children with disabilities,* Indian children, neglected or delinquent children, and *young children in need of reading assistance*" (p. 16, italics added) emphasizes a basic skills–phonics panacea for young children's literacy to the exclusion of other potentially responsive efforts.

Of course, civil rights is about valued societal access and full citizenship, not the mandating of a singular professional ideology for instruction. What I have learned in observing the literate development of young children commonly cast as hopelessly aliterate or subliterate is that the path to critical engagement with visual, orthographic, and tactile sign systems involves a range of imaginative approaches grounded always on a deeply local sense of the learner. In this way, we will recognize the child's symbolic presence, capacity to construct narratives, and potential to engage sign systems, and we will foster the child's citizenship in the inclusive early childhood literate community.

References

Adams, M.J. (1990). *Beginning to read: Thinking and learning about print.* Cambridge, MA: MIT Press.

Adams, M.J. (2001). Alphabetic anxiety and explicit, systematic phonics instruction: A cognitive science perspective. In S.B. Neuman & D.K. Dickinson (Eds.), *Handbook of early literacy research* (pp. 66–80). New York: Guilford Press.

Adams, M.J., Foorman, B.R., Lundberg, I., & Beeler, T. (1998). *Phonemic awareness in young children: A classroom curriculum.* Baltimore: Paul H. Brookes Publishing Co.

American Psychiatric Association (APA). (2004). *Diagnostic and statistical manual of mental disorders* (4th ed., text rev.). Washington, DC: Author.

Ashton-Warner, S. (1963). *Teacher.* New York: Simon & Schuster.

Bakhtin, M.M. (1986). *Speech genres and other late essays.* Austin: University of Texas Press.

Bauman, M., & Kemper, T.L. (Eds.). (1995). *The neurobiology of autism.* Baltimore: The Johns Hopkins University Press.

Bianculli, D. (1992). *Teleliteracy: Taking television seriously.* New York: Continuum.

Biklen, D. (2000). Constructing inclusion: Lessons from critical disability narratives. *International Journal of Inclusive Education, 4,* 337–353.

Biklen, D., & Burke, J. (2006). Presuming competence. *Equity and Excellence in Education, 39,* 166–175.

Biklen, D., & Rosetti, Z. (Producers). (2005). *My classic life as an artist: A portrait of Larry Bissonnette* [Video documentary]. (Available from Syracuse University School of Education, Syracuse, NY)

Bissonnette, L. (2005). Letters ordered through typing produce the story of an artist stranded on the island of autism. In D. Biklen (Ed.), *Autism and the myth of the person alone.* New York: New York University Press.

Bogdan, R., & Biklen, S.K. (2003). *Qualitative research for education: An introduction to theory and methods.* Boston: Allyn & Bacon.

Braddy, N. (1933). *Anne Sullivan Macy: The story behind Helen Keller.* New York: Doubleday.

Broderick, A., & Kasa-Hendrickson, C. (2001). "Say just one word at first": The emergence of reliable speech in a student labeled with autism. *Journal of The Association for Persons with Severe Handicaps (JASH), 26,* 13–24.

Brown v. Board of Education, 347 U.S. 483 (1954).

Buckley, S.J. (1984). The influence of family variables on children's progress on Portage. In A. Dessent (Ed.), *What is important about Portage?* (pp. 21–28) Windsor: NFER-Nelson.

Buckley, S.J. (1985). Attaining basic educational skills: Reading, writing, and number. In D. Lane & B. Stratford (Eds.), *Current approaches to Down's syndrome* (pp. 315–344). New York: Praeger.

Buckley, S.J. (1995). Teaching children with Down syndrome to read and write. In L. Nadel & D. Rosenthal (Eds.), *Down syndrome: Living and learning in the community* (pp. 158–169). New York: Wiley-Liss.

Buckley, S.J. (2006). *Literacy and young children with Down syndrome.* Paper presented at the Ninth World Down Syndrome Congress, Vancouver, BC, Canada.

Burke, J. (2005, November). *Learning from the local: Insider knowledge, literacy, & disability.* Presentation at the annual conference of TASH, Milwaukee, WI.

Burke, J. (2007, May). *The ideal school: How one small symbol of punctuation can change lives.* Presentation in Literacy, Inclusion, and Disability [CFE 600], School of Education, Department of Cultural Foundations, Syracuse, NY.

Carey, J. (2000) Preface. In C. Nolan, *Under the eye of the clock.* New York: Arcade.

Cecil, L. (1998). *Noah and the space ark.* Minneapolis, MN: Carolrhoda Books.

Christelow, E. (1989). *Five little monkeys jumping on the bed.* New York: Clarion Books.

Commission on Reading. (1985). *Becoming a nation of readers: The report of the Commission on Reading.* Washington, DC: U.S. Department of Education.

Cossu, G., & Marshall, J.C. (1990). Are cognitive skills a prerequisite to learning to read and write? *Cognitive Neuropsychology, 7,* 21–40.

Cossu, G., Rossini, F., & Marshall, J.C. (1993). When reading is acquired but phonemic awareness is not: A study of literacy in Down's syndrome. *Cognition, 46,* 129–138.

Cossu, G., Shankweiler, D., Liberman, A.M., Fowler, C., & Fisher, W.F. (1988). Awareness of phonological segments and reading ability in Italian children. *Applied Psycholinguistics, 9,* 1–16.

Crawford, P.A. (1995). Early literacy: Emerging perspectives. *Journal of Research in Childhood Education, 10,* 71–86.

Cutsforth, T.D. (1933). *The blind in school and society: A psychological study.* New York: Appleton.

Daniels, H. (1996). *An introduction to Vygotsky.* New York: Routledge.

Donnellan, A.M., & Leary, M.R. (1995). *Movement differences and diversity in autism/mental retardation: Appreciating and accommodating people with communication and behavioral challenges.* Madison, WI: DRI Press.

Duffen, L. (1979). For reading read listening. *Learning, 1,* 61–63.

Edgar, E. (1997). School reform, special education, and democracy. *Remedial and Special Education, 6,* 323–325.

Egan, K. (1999). *Children's minds, talking rabbits, and clockwork oranges.* New York: Teachers College Press.

Einhorn, L.J. (1998). *Helen Keller, public speaker: Sightless, but seen, deaf but heard.* Westport, CT: Greenwood Press.

Elementary and Secondary Education Act of 1965, PL 89-10, 20 U.S.C. §§ 6301 *et seq.*

Erickson, K.A., & Koppenhaver, D.A. (1995). Developing a literacy program for children with severe disabilities. *The Reading Teacher, 48,* 676–684.

Fernandez, R. (2001). *Imagining literacy: Rhizomes of knowledge in American culture and literature.* Austin: University of Texas Press.

Fields-Meyer, T., Duffy, T., & Arias, R. (2005, April 11). Autism: Breaking the silence. *People,* 83–86.

Freire, P. (1993). *Pedagogy of the oppressed.* New York: Continuum. (Original work published 1970)

Freire, P., & Macedo, D. (1987). *Literacy: Reading the word and the world.* South Hadley, MA: Bergin & Garvey.

Friedman, L. (1969). *Argument: The oral argument before the Supreme Court in Brown v. Board of Education of Topeka, 1952–1955.* New York: Chelsea House.

Gallas, K. (2003). *Imagination and literacy: A teacher's search for the heart of learning.* New York: Teachers College Press.

Gardner, H. (1991). *The unschooled mind: How children think and how schools should teach.* New York: Basic Books.

Geertz, C. (1983). *Local knowledge: Further essays in interpretive anthropology.* New York: Basic Books.

Goals 2000: Educate America Act of 1994, PL 103-227, 20 U.S.C. §§ 5801 *et seq.*

Good, R.H., & Kaminski, R.A. (2002). *Dynamic indicators of basic early literacy skills* (6th ed.). Eugene, OR: Institute for the Development of Educational Achievement.

Goodman, K.S. (2004, October). The children No Child Left Behind will leave behind. *Substance, 28*(10), 1–11.

Gray, L.C., & Morant, P. (2003). Reconciling indigenous knowledge with scientific assessment of soil fertility changes in southwestern Burkina Faso. *Geoderma, 111,* 425–438.

Heath, S.B. (1983). *Ways with words: Language, life, and work in communities and classrooms.* New York: Cambridge University Press.

Heath, S.B. (1986). Separating "things of the imagination" from life: Learning to read and write. In W.H. Teale & E. Sulzby (Eds.), *Emergent literacy: Writing and reading* (pp. 156–172). Norwood, NJ: Ablex.

Herszenhorn, D.M. (2004, January 7). For U.S. aid, city switches reading plan. *The New York Times,* p. F1.

Individuals with Disabilities Education Act (IDEA) of 1990, PL 101-476, 20 U.S.C. §§ 1400 *et seq.*

Individuals with Disabilities Education Improvement Act of 2004, PL 108-446, 20 U.S.C. §§ 1400 *et seq.*

International Reading Association (IRA) & National Association for the Education of Young Children (NAEYC). (1998). Learning to read and write: Developmentally appropriate practices for young children. A joint position statement of the International Reading Association and the National Association for the Education of Young Children. *Young Children, 53,* 30–46.

Johnson, A. (1903). Report of the Committee on Colonies for the Segregation of Defectives. *Proceedings of the National Conference on Charities and Corrections,* 245–254, New York.

Kasa-Hendrickson, C., Broderick, A., & Biklen, D. (Producers), & Gambell, J. (Director). (2002). *Inside the edge* [Video documentary]. (Available from Syracuse University, School of Education, Syracuse, NY)

Katims, D.S. (2000). Literacy instruction for people with mental retardation: Historical highlights and contemporary analysis. *Education & Training in Mental Retardation and Developmental Disabilities, 35,* 3–15.

Keller, H. (1908). Sense and sensibility: Part II. *Century Magazine, 75,* 773–783.

Keller, H. (1920). *The world I live in.* New York: The Century Co.

Kliewer, C. (1995). Young children's communication and literacy: A qualitative study of language in the inclusive preschool. *Mental Retardation, 33,* 143–152.

Kliewer, C. (1998a). Citizenship in the literate community: An ethnography of children with Down syndrome and the written word. *Exceptional Children, 64,* 167–180.

Kliewer, C. (1998b). *Schooling children with Down syndrome: Toward an understanding of possibility.* New York: Teachers College Press.

Kliewer, C. (1998c). The meaning of inclusion. *Mental Retardation, 36,* 317–322.

Kliewer, C., & Biklen, D. (2001). "School's not really a place for reading": A research synthesis of the literate lives of students with significant disabilities. *Journal of The Association for Persons with Severe Disabilities (JASH), 26,* 1–12.

Kliewer, C., & Biklen, D. (2007). Enacting literacy: Local understanding, significant disability, and a new frame for educational opportunity. *Teachers College Record, 109*(12).

Kliewer, C., Biklen, D., & Kasa-Hendrickson, C. (2006). Who may be literate? Disability and resistance to the cultural denial of competence. *American Educational Research Journal, 43,* 163–192.

Kliewer, C., & Drake, S. (1998). Disability, eugenics, and the current ideology of segregation: A modern moral tale. *Disability & Society, 13,* 95–113.

Kliewer, C., & Fitzgerald, L.M. (2001). Disability, schooling, and the artifacts of colonialism. *Teachers College Record, 103,* 450–470.

Kliewer, C., Fitzgerald, L.M., Meyer-Mork, J., Hartman, P., English-Sand, P., & Raschke, D. (2004). Citizenship for all in the literate community: An ethnography of young children with significant disabilities in inclusive early childhood settings. *Harvard Educational Review, 74,* 373–403.

Kliewer, C., Fitzgerald, L.M., & Raschke, D. (2001, November/December). Young children's citizenship in the literate community: Significant disability and the power of early childhood inclusion. *TASH Connections, 27*(11/12), 8–11.

Kliewer, C., & Landis, D. (1999). Individualizing literacy instruction for young children with moderate to severe disabilities. *Exceptional Children, 66,* 85–100.

Kluger, R. (1975). *Simple justice: The history of Brown v. Board of Education and black America's struggle for equality.* New York: Alfred A. Knopf.

Kluth, P., & Chandler-Olcott, K. (2008). *"A land we can share": Teaching literacy to students with autism.* Baltimore: Paul H. Brookes Publishing Co.

Koppenhaver, D.A., & Erickson, K.A. (2003). Natural emergent literacy supports for preschoolers with autism and severe communication impairments. *Topics in Language Disorders, 23,* 283–292.

Kress, G. (1997). *Before writing: Rethinking the paths to literacy.* New York: Routledge.

Kulleseid, E., & Strickland, D. (1989). *Literature, literacy, and learning.* Washington, DC: American Library Association.

Lancaster, L. (2003). Moving into literacy: How it all begins. In N. Hall, J. Larson, & J. Marsh (Eds.), *Handbook of early childhood literacy* (pp. 145–153). Thousand Oaks, CA: Sage Publications.

Landry, S.H., & Smith, K.E. (2006). The influence of parenting on emerging literacy skills. In D.K. Dickinson & S.B. Neuman (Eds.), *Handbook of early literacy research* (Vol. 2, pp. 135–148). New York: Guilford Press.

Lash, J.P. (1980). *Helen and Teacher: The story of Helen Keller and Anne Sullivan Macy.* New York: Delacorte Press.

Lippman, L., & Goldberg, I.I. (1973). *Right to education: Anatomy of the Pennsylvania case and its implications for exceptional children.* New York: Teachers College Press.

Mayer, M. (1992). *Little Critter: My trip to the hospital.* New York: Harper Collins.

McEwan, H., & Egan, K. (Eds.). (1995). *Narrative in teaching, learning, and research.* New York: Teachers College Press.

McGuinness, D. (1997). *Why our children can't read.* New York: Free Press.

Minarik, E.H. (2002). *Maurice Sendak's Little Bear: Father's flying flapjacks.* New York: Harper Festival.

Mirenda, P. (2003). "He's not really a reader...": Perspectives on supporting literacy development in individuals with autism. *Topics in Language Disorders, 23,* 271–282.

Morais, J., Carey, L., Alegria, J., & Bertelson, P. (1979). Does awareness of speech as a sequence of phones arise spontaneously? *Cognition, 7,* 323–331.

National Commission on Excellence in Education (NCEE). (1983). *A nation at risk: The imperative for educational reform.* Washington, DC: U.S. Department of Education.

National Institute of Child Health and Human Development. (2000). *Report of the National Reading Panel. Teaching children to read: An evidence-based assessment of the scientific research literature for reading instruction.* Washington, DC: U.S. Government Printing Office.

No Child Left Behind Act of 2001, PL 107-110, 115 Stat. 1425, 20 U.S.C. §§ 6301 *et seq.*

Nolan, C. (2000). *Under the eye of the clock.* New York: Arcade.

Office of the Inspector General, U.S. Department of Education. (2006). *The Reading First Program's Grant Application Process: Final inspection report.* Washington, DC: Author.

Paley, V.G. (2004). *A child's work: The importance of fantasy play.* Chicago: University of Chicago Press.

Pennsylvania Association for Retarded Children v. Commonwealth of Pennsylvania, 334 F. Supp. 1257 (E.D. Pa. 1972).

Petitto, L.A., & Marentette, P. (1991). Babbling in the manual mode: Evidence of the ontogeny of language. *Science, 251,* 1483–1496.

Piaget, J. (1973). *To understand is to invent: The future of education* (G. Roberts, Trans.). New York: Grossman.

Potter, W.J. (2004). *Theory of media literacy: A cognitive approach.* Thousand Oaks, CA: Sage Publications.

Prendergast, C. (2002). The economy of literacy: How the Supreme Court stalled the Civil Rights movement. *Harvard Educational Review, 72,* 206–229.

Rancoli, C., Ingram, K., & Kirshen, P. (2002). Reading the rains: Local knowledge and rainfall forecasting in Burkina Faso. *Society and Natural Resources, 15,* 409–428.

Razfar, A., & Gutierrez, K. (2003). Reconceptualizing early childhood literacy: The sociocultural influence. In N. Hall, J. Larson, & J. Marsh (Eds.), *Handbook of early childhood literacy* (pp. 34–47). Thousand Oaks, CA: Sage Publications.

Reading Excellence Act of 1998, PL 105-277, 112 Stat. 2681.

Resnick, D.P., & Resnick, L.B. (1977). The nature of literacy: An historical exploration. *Harvard Educational Review, 47,* 370–385.

Rey, H.A., & Rey, M. (1966). *Curious George goes to the hospital.* New York: Houghton-Mifflin.

Riessman, C.K. (2000). Analysis of personal narratives. In J.F. Gubrium & J.A. Holstein (Eds.), *Handbook of interview research* (pp. 695–710). Thousand Oaks, CA: Sage Publications.

Rogers, F. (1988). *Going to the hospital.* New York: Putnam's Sons.

Sacks, O. (1989). *Seeing voices: A journey into the world of the deaf.* Berkeley: University of California Press.

Sartre, J.P. (1961). *The psychology of imagination.* New York: Citadel.

Saunders, J., & Collins, J. (1972). *Teaching mentally handicapped children.* New York: Penny Gobby House School.

Sendak, M. (1964). *Where the wild things are.* New York: Harper & Row.

Sendak, M. (1970). *In the night kitchen.* New York: Harper & Row.

Seuss, D. (1996). *My many colored days.* New York: Knopf.

Shannon, P. (1995). *Text, lies, and videotape: Stories about life, literacy, and learning.* Portsmouth, NH: Heinemann.

Silverstein, S. (1974). *Where the sidewalk ends: The poems and drawings of Shel Silverstein.* New York: Harper & Row.

Teale, W.H., & Sulzby, E. (Eds.). (1986). *Emergent literacy: Writing and reading.* Norwood, NJ: Ablex.

U.S. Department of Education. (2006). *OSERS 27th annual report to congress on the implementation of the IDEA.* Washington, DC: Author.

Vygotsky, L.S. (1981). The genesis of higher mental functions. In J.V. Wertsch (Ed.), *The concept of activity in Soviet psychology* (J.V. Wertsch, Trans.) (pp.160–184). Armonk, ME: Sharpe Publishing.

Vygotsky, L.S. (1987). *The collected works of L.S. Vygotsky* (Vol. 1). (R.W. Rieber & J. Wollock, Eds.). New York: Plenum Press.

Vygotsky, L.S. (2003). Imagination and creativity in childhood. *Journal of Russian and East European Psychology, 42,* 7–97. (Original work published 1930)

Wagner, R.K., & Torgeson, J.K. (1987). The nature of phonological processing and its causal role in the acquisition of reading skills. *Psychological Bulletin, 101,* 192–212.

Warnock, M. (1976). *Imagination.* Berkeley: University of California Press.

Weikum, W.M., Vouloumanos, A., Navarra, J., Soto-Faraco, S., Sebastián-Gallés, S., & Werker, J.F. (2007). Visual language discrimination in infancy. *Science, 316*, 1159–1165.

Whitehurst, G.J., & Lonigan, C.J. (2001). Emergent literacy: Development from prereaders to readers. In S.B. Neuman & D.K. Dickinson (Eds.), *Handbook of early literacy research* (pp. 11–29). New York: Guilford Press.

Wojahn, R.H. (2006). *Evan early.* Bethesda, MD: Woodbine House Press.

Zill, N., & Resnick, G. (2006). Emergent literacy of low-income children in Head Start: Relationships with child and family characteristics, program factors, and classroom quality. In D.K. Dickinson & S.B. Neuman (Eds.), *Handbook of early literacy research* (Vol. 2, pp. 347–374). New York: Guilford Press.

Index

Page numbers followed by *t* indicate tables.